Consumer-Directed Healthcare and Its Implications for Providers

6/06
39.00
Direct

Your board, staff, or clients may also benefit from this book's insight. For more information on quantity discounts, contact the Health Administration Press Marketing Manager at (312) 424-9470.

This publication is intended to provide accurate and authoritative information in regard to the subject matter covered. It is sold, or otherwise provided, with the understanding that the publisher is not engaged in rendering professional services. If professional advice or other expert assistance is required, the services of a competent professional should be sought.

The statements and opinions contained in this book are strictly those of the author(s) and do not represent the official positions of the author's employer, of the American College of Healthcare Executives, or of the Foundation of the American College of Healthcare Executives.

Library of Congress Cataloging-in-Publication Data

Bonney, Robert.
     Consumer-directed healthcare and its implications for providers / Robert S. Bonney.
          p. cm.
     Includes bibliographical references.
     ISBN-10: 1-56793-241-X (alk. paper)
     ISBN-13: 978-1-56793-241-6 (alk. paper)
          1. Health planning—Citizen participation. 2. Insurance, Health. 3. Medical economics. 4. Consumer
     satisfaction. I. Title.

RA394.B66 2005
362.1'068—dc22

                                                                                            2005046359

The paper used in this publication meets the minimum requirements of American National Standard for Information Sciences—Permanence of Paper for Printed Library Materials, ANSI Z39.48-1984. ⊚ ™

Acquisitions editor: Janet Davis; Project manager: Joyce Sherman; Layout editor: Amanda Karvelaitis;
Cover design: Betsy Pérez

Health Administration Press
A division of the Foundation of the
     American College of Healthcare Executives
1 North Franklin Street, Suite 1700
Chicago, IL 60606-4425
(312) 424-2800

CHAPTER 1

How Did We Get to this New Marketplace?

The marketplace is now ripe for new consumer-directed products designed to engage patients economically in their healthcare decisions.

Many factors have contributed to the double-digit increases in healthcare premiums experienced annually by employers and employees since 2001 (Fuhrmans 2004). At least four major factors have contributed to these increases: federal government policy, the economy, the decreased supply of physicians and hospital beds, and the cost of drugs.

FEDERAL GOVERNMENT POLICY

When the Balanced Budget Act of 1997 was implemented, significant cuts were made in payments to hospitals and ▶

physicians. This led hospitals to shift their cost increases to the commercial insurers to make up for government reductions, in essence creating an indirect tax on the purchasers of commercial insurance to support Medicare. The commercial insurers then passed these increases on to the employers.

In addition, health savings account legislation was passed in 2003, encouraging employers to offer these accounts to their employees as part of their health benefits. Legislation was already in place permitting employees to put money into a pretax fund to pay for healthcare expenses, but the employees lost whatever they did not spend from the fund for that year. This discouraged some employers from participating in the program. Medical savings accounts, which function like individual retirement accounts except that they are limited to medical costs, were also implemented. But as with health savings accounts, they did not grow as hoped because of the restrictions on the use of these accounts (e.g., use was restricted to employers with 50 or fewer employees). Health savings accounts were designed to address many of the concerns of the prior legislative initiatives, and it is anticipated that many employers will

use this vehicle as they look for alternative ways to finance healthcare benefits for their employees. This opportunity allows insurers to introduce consumer-directed products more easily into their portfolio. Table 1 compares the available options.

ECONOMY

Another factor at work in this environment of dramatically increased premiums is the economy. In good economic times, and in particular periods of low unemployment as was experienced in the 1990s, employers are reluctant to pass on increases in healthcare premiums to their employees for fear of losing those employees. During low unemployment periods the cost of not having a sufficient supply of highly qualified employees becomes a greater cost to business than passing on the increases in healthcare costs to the employees. Toward the end of the 1990s, as the economy softened, some employers became more willing to pass on increases in costs to employees, as a more ready workforce was available from which to recruit. In addition, employers were more willing to experiment with different benefit programs. This combination of factors creates a

Table 1. Attributes of Various Health Benefit Accounts

	Health Savings Account	Flexible Spending Account	Health Reimbursement Arrangement	Medical Savings Account
Who is eligible?				
Small employers	Yes	Yes	Yes	Yes, if 50 or fewer employees
Large employers	Yes	Yes	Yes	No
Self-employed	Yes	No	No	Yes
What are the key requirements?				
High-deductible insurance required	Yes	No	No	Yes
Account retained by employee upon termination of employment	Yes	Yes	No, but terminated employee may be covered by plan	Yes
Who makes contributions?				
Employer contribution	Optional	Optional	Required	Optional
Employee contribution	Optional	Optional	No	Optional
Employee tax implications	Contribution is tax free	Contribution is tax free	Claim reimbursements are tax free	Contribution is deductible on 1040 form
Account prefunded by employer	No	Yes	No	No
What are some permitted uses?				
Roll unused dollars to next year	Yes	No	Yes	Yes
Reimburse IRS section 213(d) medical expenses	Yes	Yes	Yes	Yes
Pay long-term care premiums from account	Yes	No	Yes	Yes
Convert to taxable income	Yes	No	No	Yes

natural environment in which to introduce products that engage the user through more direct financial participation.

DECREASED SUPPLY OF PHYSICIANS AND HOSPITAL BEDS

During the period of rapid growth of health maintenance organizations (HMOs), providers were willing to offer pricing concessions in return for volume, as many providers—particularly many hospitals—had surplus capacity. This led HMOs to create narrow networks and benefit plans designed to direct business to network providers in return for significantly reduced pricing. Health maintenance organizations also promised rapid turnaround of claims and no-hassle collection on the part of the provider because deductibles and coinsurance were very limited. The intent of these plans was to encourage utilization of preventive services and acute services as needed and eliminate the member/patient's disincentive to seek care.

Again, during the economic boom of the 1990s people did not like the restrictions placed on them by HMOs, and they sought to have them removed. Over time, to make their

products more attractive, many HMOs broadened their networks to include as many providers as possible. They also added point-of-service products that permitted out-of-network use with higher copayments.

During this time HMOs tried a variety of methods to control utilization by providers. The most common of these was the requirement to obtain permission from the payer prior to providing certain defined services. The provider community met this approach with significant resistance. Health maintenance organizations also frequently denied payment when a service was not considered to be "medically necessary," a vague term that was subject to significantly variable interpretation. Most payers ultimately abandoned these techniques because they were costly and yielded limited results.

Finally, many health plans introduced high-deductible benefit designs to put some of the onus of medical costs on the patient. Thus the promise of the HMO to providers was eroded.

In addition, the hospital surplus capacity was significantly reduced in many markets because of hospital consolidations and closures. This reduction, coupled with the aging of the population, led to a shortage of hospital capacity in some markets. As a result, hospitals decided to toughen their negotiation with payers and were willing to terminate contracts that no longer met their financial goals. In addition, a physician shortage began to emerge in some markets. Payers needed stable networks, so in many markets, payers were forced to pay providers more for their services or run the risk of losing market share.

DRUG COSTS

Health plans were experiencing rapid increases in drug costs during the 1990s. The typical benefit design was a $10 copayment for generic drugs and a $20 copayment for drugs on the health plan's formulary. If the drug was not on the formulary, a doctor could go through an appeal process to try to get the drug approved. The HMOs' denials of drug coverage often angered doctors and patients and contributed to the bad reputation that HMOs received. The ineffectiveness of this process led to the development of a three-tiered benefit design whereby a patient would pay $10 for a generic drug, $20 for a drug on the formulary, and $30 for a drug off the formulary. This scheme was well received by employers and patients, and the HMO was no longer the "bad guy" for denying coverage of a drug. The phenomenon of allowing patients to have whatever they needed but requiring them to pay for the different choices they made was not lost on the insurance industry and is a cornerstone for the new consumer-directed products.

The marketplace is now ripe for new consumer-directed products designed to engage patients economically in their healthcare decisions. These new products require provider pricing transparency and will have implications for all providers. We discuss the major implications throughout the remainder of this book.

REFERENCE

Fuhrmans, V. 2004. "Health-Care Costs for Companies, Employees Surge." *Wall Street Journal*, September 10, A2.

What Consumer-Directed **Models** Will Emerge?

In the ideal consumer-directed product, the user would know the cost of all health services before they are provided.

The primary goal of consumer-directed products is to involve the user of healthcare in the decision-making process. The current managed care models insulate users in at least two ways. First, users are usually unaware of what a healthcare service costs. The benefit designs provided by traditional health maintenance organization (HMO) or preferred provider organization (PPO) products historically do not provide incentives for users to learn about the cost of services provided because many are linked to fixed copayments. For example, to get ▶

outpatient physical therapy, a user might have to pay $20 per visit, regardless of the network facility where he or she receives the treatment. Yet the cost to the health plan likely varies depending on the rates that were negotiated between the different providers and the health plan. Consumer-directed products seek to make prices transparent to the user. Thus, in the ideal consumer-directed product, the user would know the cost of all health services before they are provided.

The second way users are insulated from the cost is by their own reliance on their physician to direct their care. Users of healthcare look to their physician to direct where they should get their care, and they assume that their physician knows the best place to get the care they need. While this may be true, often the physician is unaware of the cost differences to the user of these referral recommendations. To moderate this strong physician influence and involve the user in referral decisions, the new consumer-directed models attempt to provide users with information to assist them in determining the right place to get care (from the payer's perspective) at the best price.

There are many variations on the theme of consumer-directed

Figure 1. Consumer-Directed Models

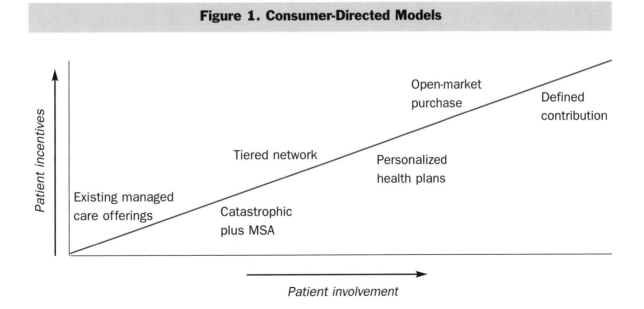

products. Figure 1 illustrates the range of products and the amount of involvement of the patient in making decisions. Each model uniquely affects the nature of the network, the benefit design, the cost of care, and the amount of incentives available to the patient. This linear, two-dimensional chart is overly simplistic, as the variations are such that these products could appear anywhere on or off the line, but it helps to point out the various models that are emerging or have the potential to emerge.

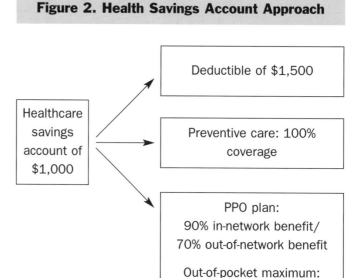

Figure 2. Health Savings Account Approach

HIGH-DEDUCTIBLE PLANS

A high-deductible plan is one in which the users pay the first costs up to a certain amount out of their own pocket before their health benefit plan takes over paying the costs of care. For example, in a $2,000 deductible plan, the user is responsible for the first $2,000 of expenses covered under the policy before the policy begins to pay.

The consumer-directed version of the high-deductible plan would contain a health savings account (HSA) or medical savings account (MSA) option. Under this approach the employer could contribute a portion of the deductible into the HSA,

and the employee could contribute the balance up to the amount of the full deductible. Then the HSA could be used to cover the deductible costs. The amount in the HSA that is not used would then roll over for use by the user the next year. Usually the employer elects to provide preventive services (e.g., annual physical exam, PAP smear, mammography) as a fully covered benefit and not charge it against the HSA to encourage participation. As shown in Figure 2, a PPO benefit plan would provide coverage once the deductible is met.

It is important to note that most high-deductible plans are usually offered on the health insurer's PPO platform because these plans have fewer restrictions from a regulatory point of view than an HMO product has. The implications of the plan being on the PPO platform rather than the HMO platform are discussed more fully in Chapter 4.

Most of the major payer companies have developed high-deductible products that use MSAs or HSAs together with their PPO products. In addition, companies that specialize in this type of benefit plan, such as Definity.com and Lumenos.com, use MSAs or HSAs and lease existing PPO networks.

A significant amount of education is needed to help the patient understand how a high-deductible plan works. Several companies are making available cost and quality information for employees to consider when selecting a provider. These companies use whatever data are available to arrive at an estimated cost for a procedure or service. They also provide either quality information themselves or links to web sites that offer this information.

TIERED NETWORKS

A tiered network is essentially one that requires patients to pay different levels of copayments or coinsurance for the same type of providers in the network based on some cost/quality ranking by the payer. This is not a new concept. Many health plans have designed their benefits to encourage patients to use one outpatient service over another, for example, using an urgent care center instead of a hospital emergency department. This concept is being expanded to include payment-level requirements for hospitals, physicians, and outpatient service providers. There are many variations of tiered networks being used, including tiered hospital networks and tiered physician networks.

Tiered Hospital Networks
BASED ON COST TO THE HEALTH PLAN. Patients' out-of-pocket expenses, such as hospital copayments and coinsurance, vary depending on the hospital selected. The underlying basis for the copayment differential in most health plans is cost to the health plan, with quality indicators presented for patient information. For example, the list of hospitals might look like section A of Table 2.

The higher the number of stars, the higher is the quality ranking.

The same model is being used for outpatient services such as

Table 2. Tiered Hospital Network

A. Based on Cost to the Health Plan

Hospital	Copayment	Quality Ranking
A	$100/day	****
B	$100/day	**
C	$200/day	*
D	$300/day	***

B. Based on Meeting Certain Quality Indicators

Hospital	Copayment	Quality Indicators Met
A	None	95 percent or more
B	$100/day	85 percent to 94 percent
C	$200/day	75 percent to 84 percent
D	$300/day	<75 percent

ambulatory surgery. Those choosing to get outpatient surgery at a hospital might have to pay a higher copayment than if they went to a freestanding center.

BASED ON MEETING CERTAIN QUALITY INDICATORS.

A model similar to that contingent on the cost to the health plan could be developed based solely on meeting selected quality indicators. Under this model the selected indicators, if met, would also have the impact of lowering cost for the health plan. The copayment to the patient would vary depending on the success a hospital has in meeting the indicators. A sample breakdown of this model appears in section B of Table 2.

Under this model the cost to the health plan is not a consideration in the amount of copayment to the patient. This type of model might be more acceptable to hospitals with large indigent populations and/or large teaching programs that are usually disadvantaged by tiered hospital networks.

Some plans define quality and then present a quality index or ranking of providers to their members. At least four large national payers' web sites, accessible only by their members, ask a series of questions as to what is important to the patient in selecting a hospital. Patients are asked to indicate their preferences regarding such factors as distance from their home, the hospital's mortality and morbidity data, and cost to the patient. Then the payers provide a ranking of the hospitals that best meet the patients' criteria. This way, the payer attempts not only to provide information to its members but also, and more importantly, to influence their selection of hospitals within the network.

Tiered Physician Networks

In addition to using tiers for physicians that are similar to hospitals, at least one plan allows physicians to select the tier in which they want to participate. Physicians can select how much they want to be paid as a percentage of Medicare, say 90 percent, 110 percent, or 130 percent. The physicians choosing the lowest reimbursement percentage will be in the tier assigned the lowest copayment rate, those choosing the next lowest percentage will be assigned the next lowest copayment tier, and those choosing the highest percentage will be assigned the highest tier.

Some health plans may tier physicians on the basis of how their costs compare with those of their peers. These plans would take into consideration all costs associated with the physician. Thus, physicians who practice at high-cost hospitals, even if they have a lower average length of stay than that of their peers, might be in a higher copayment tier. Other plans may just look at physician costs in making the comparison to determine the copayment tier.

SCHEDULE OF COVERED SERVICES

Historically, certain services have been carved out of the contracts with hospitals and provided by specialty contractors. For example, most health plans carve out mental health services and contract with a mental health management company to provide these services for a fixed, per-member, per-month cost.

Some health plans are considering carving certain services from their network and permitting patients to go wherever they want for these services. These plans are returning to a practice of creating a schedule of certain services on their covered services list and limiting the amount of payment they will make for these services. For example, cardiovascular surgery is covered to a maximum of $15,000. The member is free to go wherever he or she wants to go, but the insurer is limiting what he or she pays to $15,000. Thus, the significance of being served by an out-of-network provider is greatly reduced. Payers are already testing this benefit design with respect to the pharmacy benefit. Under this model, drugs are divided into therapeutic classes. A fixed amount of coverage is available to the member based on the class into which the drug falls. The member is responsible for the difference.

PERSONALIZED HEALTH PLANS

Personalized health plans take two basic forms. The first allows the purchaser to customize his or her benefits and/or copayments and deductibles according to individual need and paying a premium for only those services that the purchaser wants to buy. For example, the purchaser who does not want to buy coverage for obstetrics services might be permitted to opt out of this coverage, resulting in a lower premium. Or the buyer could choose a high-deductible plan with higher copayments for physician and drug coverage, again lowering the premium significantly. Providers are usually limited to predetermined networks from which the purchaser chooses.

The second option gives purchasers the ability to customize not only their benefits but also their provider network. Premiums are then calculated based on the selection of both individual providers and hospitals that the purchaser has chosen for their network together with the selected benefit design.

This second option, pioneered by Vivius.com, allows purchasers to select their primary care provider and certain specialists in some 30 categories. Purchasers make a selection of one provider in each category, including a hospital. They can then change the providers and determine the impact on their premium and repeat this process until they arrive at a customized premium and network to suit their individual needs. This type of customized care plan becomes very narrow for in-network services; a PPO or other high-deductible product is used for all out-of-network services.

OPEN-MARKET APPROACHES

Several other models either have emerged or might emerge in a consumer-directed environment, including a "name your price" approach; spot-market pricing; discount cards; and a "buy one, get one free" model. Each presents the provider with new challenges and opportunities.

Name Your Price
For those purchasers who have a fixed dollar limit on their benefit—say $15,000 for open-heart surgery—a

product that permits them to shop online for a hospital that offers an all-inclusive price (including physicians' fees) might be attractive. Under this model the patient might post all of his or her medical information according to a predetermined format together with the price he or she is willing to pay. The hospital and surgeon would review the data and agree to perform the necessary procedure for the fixed amount. In addition to price, they could communicate back to the potential patient their quality data and other information that might lead the patient to choose their services. The hospital might even make hotel and other arrangements for the patient's family.

Spot-Market Pricing

Under the spot-market pricing model the prospective patient might post online his or her medical history according to a predetermined format and request an all-inclusive (including physicians' fees) bid from a hospital. Hospitals would then have the opportunity to compete on the basis of both price and quality to provide the needed services.

Discount Cards

A noninsurance product—the discount card—is making its way into the healthcare marketplace. For a small monthly fee a purchaser can gain access to a network of providers that will discount their services. The holders of these cards are allowed access to many hospital and physician contracts through leased PPO arrangements.

Despite their appeal, discount cards can cause confusion. Say the patient presents his or her card upon admission or a visit to the physician. The card has the leased PPO's logo on it, and the physician's office or hospital admitting clerk assumes that it is an insurance card, only to find out when the remittance advice is received from the health plan that the patient has a 100 percent copayment of the amount contracted through the leased PPO. Providers must be alert to these emerging products and ensure that collection is initiated prior to providing nonemergent services or run the risk of an increase in their uncollectible accounts.

Buy One, Get One Free

As foreign as this might sound in healthcare, physicians or hospitals might offer a patient the opportunity to get a second procedure free when he or she purchases the first. For example, an orthopedic surgeon who is just starting a practice in a new market might be willing to offer two knee procedures for the price of one if the patients requiring bilateral knee procedures can have them both done during the same operation. Of course, this offer could not be made to Medicare or Medicaid patients but could potentially be made to commercially insured, consumer-directed patients.

Although this type of approach is not likely to emerge as a significant initiative, it is mentioned to show that there are all kinds of possibilities when patients have a significant financial stake in selecting their providers.

DEFINED CONTRIBUTION MODEL

Currently most health benefit plans are defined benefits plans whereby an employer selects the benefits to be offered and pays all or a portion of the premium for the employee. Under *defined contribution plans* the employer makes a contribution of a specific amount of money into a fund each month, and the employee is free to use that fund to pay for his or her healthcare needs, including insurance premiums.

Pure defined contribution plans are not likely to emerge anytime soon, for several reasons. The first barrier is the inability to manage adverse selection. *Adverse selection* occurs in insurance when people who use more healthcare services purchase comprehensive coverage and those who do not use healthcare services purchase limited coverage. This is probably the biggest problem preventing defined contribution plans from emerging. The concept of insurance is to spread the risk across all risk categories. When adverse selection occurs, risk is not spread. Over time those purchasing comprehensive coverage are not able to pay for it because it becomes too expensive: those who use limited services subsidize those who use comprehensive services and they are no longer part of the pricing equation.

Under pure defined contribution plans, adverse selection is unavoidable over the long term. Adverse selection is also a detrimental factor for cooperatives that purchase health insurance. The theory is that a very large group has more purchasing power and can get better rates. This is a seemingly logical approach, but it too lends itself to adverse selection. Those groups that can buy insurance cheaper on their own will do so. Over time, those remaining in the group will tend to be those at higher risk.

The insurer will price for this risk, and eventually the group will become a high-cost group.

Another reason that pure defined contribution is not likely to emerge as a dominant model is the paternal nature of many employers. Employers fear that, because healthcare is very complex, most employees when left to their own devices will not make appropriate selections over the long term. Indeed, consumer-directed products are complicated and require significant education of the workforce to be successful. Employers' fears about the average worker being able to understand the nuances and wanting to take the time to understand their benefits is likely valid. If we think about how much time we spend (assuming we are healthy and do not currently need complex healthcare services)

reviewing our current policies and trying to understand them prior to making a purchase, we would probably agree with these employers. Many purchasers tend to assume that coverage will be present when they need it and do not take the time to understand what coverage they are buying at the time of purchase.

Finally, a lesser problem that multisite employers experience needs to be managed: whether or not the amount of the contribution made to the fund should be the same for all locations or should vary depending on the cost of living in each area.

Now that we have reviewed the various models that are likely to emerge under a consumer-directed approach, in the next chapter we will spend some time looking at how an organization might position itself to achieve maximum benefits.

CHAPTER 3

How Can I Best Position My Organization?

The critical first step for a hospital or provider in preparing for consumer-directed plans is positioning the organization to be wanted by the payer.

NEED FOR A STRATEGY

The first step for any health system, hospital, or provider group is to position itself to be successful. Once it has developed a competitive advantage and is desired by the purchasers of healthcare, it is ready to develop a consumer-directed strategy.

Competitive Advantage: You Have to Be Wanted

The pricing transparency of consumer-directed healthcare products will finally put to the test whether an organization ▶

has a true competitive advantage in the healthcare marketplace—one for which the patient is willing to pay more. The critical first step for a hospital or provider in preparing for consumer-directed plans is positioning the organization to be wanted by the payer. Many factors contribute to this positioning, including the following:

- The extent to which the organization is payer friendly
- The willingness to collaborate with the payer
- The location and number of clinical sites
- The scope and uniqueness of services offered
- The physician network and its participants' willingness to contract with the payer
- The organization's image
- The cost of the services to the health plan
- The willingness to measure and report quality data

The second critical step under consumer-directed healthcare is the positioning of the organization to be wanted by the patient. Many of the same factors that contribute to a payer's desire to contract with the organization apply to the patient's willingness to choose it. However, one factor listed above—cost of services—takes on an additional emphasis. Under the traditional health maintenance organization or preferred provider organization model, the patient chose any hospital or physician and paid the same price out of his or her pocket regardless of the cost to the health plan. Under the new model of consumer-directed healthcare, with high-deductible plans leading the way, the cost to the consumer becomes an issue. This is particularly true for lower-cost services needed before the high deductible is met. A critical question that an organization or provider needs to ask is whether people are willing to pay more to utilize your services than those of your competitor. If the answer is yes, then a true competitive advantage exists.

WHAT STRATEGIC APPROACH MIGHT AN ORGANIZATION TAKE?

There are many different approaches that an organization can take toward dealing with consumer-directed products. Which approach to choose depends on the market conditions facing the organization. Three broad approaches are discussed below: do nothing, position the organization for the eventual emergence of consumer-directed products, and embrace consumer-directed products.

Do Nothing

Doing nothing is always an option. If the organization believes that the models identified in Chapter 2 are not likely to have a long life or to emerge in its market at all, then the strategy of maintaining the status quo may be a good one. Organizations in this situation should continue to focus on developing their competitive advantage. This strategy might be appropriate where a hospital or provider group has a near monopoly, such as a sole community hospital in a rural market.

Position the Organization for the Emergence of Consumer-Directed Products

Organizations in highly competitive markets or those that believe that consumer-directed products are likely to come to their market should begin to position themselves to thrive with these products. The steps necessary to achieve success vary depending on the type of products that one believes will emerge or will be sustained in the long term. Several opportunities

exist for better positioning, regardless of the type of product that might emerge.

PRICES. Hospitals are ill equipped to provide charge information to patients requesting it prior to services being rendered. Because deductibles and coinsurance amounts are based on *contracted rates* and not billed charges, it is important that a hospital or freestanding center have a system to provide appropriate pricing information to inquiring customers based on their actual health plan, or suffer a loss of business to those hospitals that can.

Consider this example: A patient needs magnetic resonance imaging of the shoulder and calls the hospital to inquire about the cost. Hospital A looks it up on the hospital's charge master and quotes the charge of $1,500. Freestanding Imaging Center B provides its charge of $800. Hospital C executes the following procedure:

1. All inquiries are routed to a central location where the staff are trained to provide pricing information.
2. The central department staff determine what insurance company and what specific product and benefit plan the patient has.

3. They look up the contracted rate and find that it is $675.

4. They provide the $675 rate to the patient, identify the amount of the coinsurance (if the patient has met his or her deductible) that will be required, and either fax or e-mail confirmation of all of the information received and the rate. This confirmation contains the appropriate disclaimers mentioning that charges change if services different from those quoted are provided (often the patient indicates a procedure different from what has been ordered). In addition, the department can provide information to the caller that differentiates the facility from the competition.

Because the patient is paying for the service himself or herself and no difference in quality is apparent, the patient chooses Hospital C. The rate quoted depends on the specific rates that the insurance company has negotiated with the hospital, not the "list price" that is quoted by the other hospitals. Hospital C also takes the opportunity to sell its services in the event that it is not the lowest price, as described in step 4.

Many hospitals have used their competitive advantage in the market to obtain excellent rates from payers in the outpatient area. In fact, hospitals often structure their contracts with payers with the aim to make their profit margin from outpatient services. Under consumer-directed plans, hospitals will need to consider reversing that approach. They will want to develop their payer contracts such that the rates paid to hospitals by the payers for outpatient services are similar to what the payer pays competitive outpatient centers in the market. If they do not contract with payers in this way, hospitals will run the risk of losing outpatient business. They will want to consider a contract-neutral change by pricing inpatient services higher and outpatient services lower, making certain that the aggregate payments remain the same.

In addition, hospitals should be aware that most consumer-directed products will be governed by an insurance license rather than an HMO license. Thus, if the hospital believes that there is likely to be growth in these types of products, it will cautiously evaluate whether it makes sense to move to one fee schedule for all products as many health plans are advocating. Doing so might result in lower payment over time as health plans shift business from their HMO product to their preferred provider organization product.

COLLECTIONS. With the increase in the amount of payment required from the patient, the amount of bad debt incurred by a hospital or provider will likely increase absent strong policies to manage bad debt. It will be incumbent on hospitals to develop systems to collect the coinsurance and deductibles prior to providing nonemergent services if they expect to limit the growth in bad debt.

Hospitals will want to evaluate their policies regarding collecting deposits to cover coinsurance and deductibles prior to admission of a patient for nonemergent services. Advising the patient during the preadmission process of this requirement will prevent any misunderstanding by the patient.

The payers have a responsibility in this area as well. They need to develop systems such that providers and hospitals know the amount left before a patient meets his or her deductible and/or out-of-pocket maximum. This procedure is necessary to limit the amount of refunds that providers will have to make later because they collect a deposit when they are unaware that these limits have been met.

QUALITY MEASUREMENT AND REPORTING. One of the central components of the consumer-directed approach is to provide patients with not only price information but also quality information. The difficulty for the provider or hospital is that there is little consistency in reporting by payer; each payer chooses to identify quality using its own criteria. Some use raw data; some use risk-adjusted data; some consider cost, whereas others do not; some use state all-payer data, whereas others use only Medicare data. Some payers refer their members to web sites that provide this information, such as http://www.leapfroggroup.org/ (the Leapfrog Group, a consortium of businesses that buy healthcare whose aim is to ensure healthcare quality) and http://www.healthgrades.com/ (HealthGrades, an Internet service that grades the performance of U.S. healthcare providers).

Other plans use their own proprietary systems to help patients make their selections. It is clear that until there is an accepted universal standard to measure quality, hospitals need to decide how they are going to respond to all of the information being presented. At a minimum hospitals and physicians need to know what data are being used by

CONSIDER THIS

Pay those staff who register patients a bonus for collecting the deductibles/ copayments/ coinsurance for nonemergent services at the time of the patient's registration.

CONSIDER THIS

Most hospitals have made significant efforts to bill the health plan as soon as possible after the patient is discharged to improve cash flow. Hospitals might want to rethink this practice for patients with high-deductible plans. They could instead wait until the end of the timely filing period before filing the claim. This way other claims that have been filed earlier will be counted against the deductible, and the hospital will have less exposure for collection from the patient.

the payers and how the payers are representing them to their members. As part of the contracting process with health plans, providers should seek to obtain a dummy member identification number so that they can use the payer's web site to understand how patients are being directed. They should also seek access to post a comment on the payer's web site whenever their data are displayed so as to clarify that data.

Whether or not you believe that consumer-directed healthcare will make it to your market, it is very likely that health plans will start to try to influence their member selection through their web site provider search engines. Thus, it is important that you know how the search engines work and how the payers portray your organization.

TIERED PRICING MODELS. The tiered pricing models present different opportunities for physicians and hospitals. Physicians or physician groups that have full practices but have contracts with some very low-paying health plans might view a tiered pricing model as a way of transitioning some of their business to a higher-paying practice. They would seek to enter into contracts

that provide a higher level of reimbursement than they are currently receiving, and they would advise their patients in the low-paying plan that they intend to terminate the plan and provide them with a list of alternatives. Once they start receiving patients from the new plan they would terminate a low-paying health plan, and their patient population would transition to a higher reimbursement level.

Hospitals would likely begin their evaluation of whether to participate with these plans by reviewing their cost profile with the payer. If the pricing structure is on the lower end, the hospital would probably be placed in the tier with the lowest copayment requirements to provide a financial incentive to use the hospital. If the pricing structure paid the hospital higher rates, it would likely be placed in higher tiers and thus would not want to participate with these plans.

Hospitals are paid higher rates because of a perceived competitive advantage. The health plan believes that the hospital needs to be in its network to attract business and is willing to pay more to get that hospital. In addition, higher-cost hospitals may have medical education programs and/or care for a higher percentage of the indigent population. Under a tiered approach the health plan is able to maintain the hospital in its network but at the same time direct business to lower-cost hospitals.

A public policy question arises regarding this model: If hospital prices become transparent and patients begin making decisions largely based on price, who will pay for indigent care or medical education? Under the current model the commercial customer pays a share of the higher costs associated with indigent care and/or medical education. If forced to compete on price, hospitals with large teaching programs or large indigent populations may have to reorient their organization by either reducing the amount of medical education they provide or rationing the amount of indigent care they provide, or both. Often higher indigent care accompanies medical education programs because they use resident help to provide the care. These programs are not likely to survive if patients start choosing hospitals based on cost, as hospitals will need to reduce costs to compete with those whose prices are significantly lower. For this model to be widely accepted without negatively affecting medical

education and indigent care programs, the federal or state government will need to step in and subsidize these programs.

What do you do when a health plan introduces a tiered product in your market if your health system contains the marquis hospital (i.e., the one that every health plan believes it needs to sell its product) or if your hospital is the marquis hospital and is receiving a high rate of reimbursement from a payer? Recall what happened with tiered copayments for prescriptions. It did not take very long (five years or so) before it was the standard benefit design. The same could easily happen with tiered health plan networks. Not to participate with the tiered product while continuing to participate with other products offered by the health plan allows the health plan to introduce the tiered product and move business from its existing product to the new product over time in a smooth transition. Not to participate with all products (not just the tiered product) offered by that payer creates disruption to the payer's network and may cause the payer to rethink its strategy. Nonparticipation in all products offered by a payer only works if the health system or hospital has a real competitive advantage, one where the health plan must have it in the network to succeed in the long term.

HEALTH PLAN WEB SITES.

As mentioned earlier in this chapter, health plans are providing online support to their members through their web sites. These tools direct members to providers based on various criteria. For example, a health plan could direct patients to low-cost providers in their network that also meet the members' other selection criteria. In this way the health plans can create a network within a network and direct members to selected hospitals within the subnetwork.

Hospitals that are the market leaders or that charge higher rates will need to evaluate their approach to these plans. Hospitals historically have given pricing considerations to health plans that drive volume to their hospital. In addition, the marquis hospitals have been able to command higher rates from the health plans based on their market position. Thus, the makeup of the health plan's network (i.e., the other hospitals in the network) and the ability of the network to drive volume to these hospitals through its benefit designs has been a criterion

that hospitals use when establishing their prices with health plans.

If the health plan contains the marquis hospital but patients are being directed away from that hospital, in effect the health plan has the best of all worlds. It is able to include the marquis hospital in its network when it markets its product but direct members not to use the higher-cost marquis hospital when they seek services.

Hospitals will need to evaluate whether past contracting approaches are still valid. Among the questions they should ask are the following:

- Should a health plan get the current discount rates when it is directing business away from the contracted hospital?
- Should the hospital change its pricing criteria to be based on actual volume received rather than the network's ability to direct members to stay within the network?
- Should the hospital participate with health plans that direct members to one contracted provider over another based on price?

PERSONALIZED HEALTH PLANS.

The health plan that gives members the ability to select their individual providers and create a customized network is the ultimate network-within-a-network model. Here the health plan wants to contract with as many providers as possible and is willing to pay those providers whatever they want. The premium that the member pays ultimately depends on the member's network selection. Under this model patients are directed to various providers at the time they enroll in the product by changing the premium that the member will pay. Each member ends up with a customized network to meet his or her budget and health needs.

This model will likely have greater appeal to physicians with busy practices who want to increase their patient mix of higher-paying patients. Because a particular physician's fee schedule is likely to have minimal impact on the ultimate premium that a patient pays, a doctor may be able to charge a high rate and participate with these plans and still be selected by the member.

These models, however, once again create a potential problem for the marquis hospital. Because hospital rates are arguably the most influential factor affecting health premiums, the marquis hospital will probably not be selected as often as other hospitals.

Thus, the marquis hospital or the hospital with the higher cost profile has to evaluate its participation with these types of plans. By participating, the marquis hospital helps the health plan market its product because that hospital is part of the network. The key question is whether it receives the promised volume. While it will get patients that are willing to pay more, it needs to evaluate the impact on its current business. If this model becomes accepted in the local market and members begin to switch to it from other health plans that do not create networks within networks, will the marquis hospital be better off or worse off as a result?

OPEN-MARKET MODELS. The open-market models offer an opportunity for those hospitals that have surplus capacity, know with some degree of certainty their costs, and are willing to put the infrastructure in place to efficiently administer them. It is anticipated that these models will emerge for high cost, highly specialized services and will require that hospital and physician fees be combined in the pricing of those services. Services that would lend themselves to this type of pricing are high-cost, complex coronary procedures, orthopedic procedures, or transplant services. Hospitals will need to develop a mechanism for responding to patient requests for pricing, as well as mechanisms for collecting and dividing the all-inclusive fees associated with the procedure.

NAME YOUR PRICE. In the name-your-price model the patient indicates how much he or she can pay, and the hospital decides if it can or wants to provide the service for the amount. There is a degree of risk in this model for those choosing to participate. Guidelines would need to be established in the event that an unexpected complication occurs that requires special care. Communication to the potential patient carefully and clearly explaining the hospital's policies on dealing with these situations would need to be developed.

Assuming that these administrative issues can be satisfactorily addressed, participating with this model may be a way to generate additional volume for the hospital with surplus capacity. In addition, it may be a way to attract patients from outside the region to utilize the hospital's services.

A potentially challenging aspect of participation in a name-your-price model is determining your price point. You do not want to set it below that of other health plans with which you contract. To do so would invite their demand for lower pricing when they find out that you have provided a better price to a single patient when they provide significantly more volume to your hospital. The need for a pricing policy is discussed in Chapter 4.

Embrace the Consumer-Directed Model

The third strategic approach that an organization might employ regarding consumer-directed products is to fully embrace them. This strategy could involve any or all of the following:

- Totally replacing your employee health benefits with a consumer-directed model. A total replacement product is required if the healthcare organization wants to avoid the inevitable problems of adverse selection that are created when multiple benefit offerings are available.
- Entering into an exclusive arrangement with a leading consumer-directed vendor to provide services for your employees and at the same time serve as the local network for the product.

Health systems that are the marquis system in the market might find that this strategy provides a way of competing with plans that offer consumer-directed products while limiting the network to the system providers and hospitals.

- Offering a better pricing arrangement to selected consumer-directed products in return for placing system hospitals in preferred pricing tiers and/or for directing members to system hospitals via the insurer's web site. It is important to note that if this strategy is employed, it will not likely be sustainable in the long run. Once the health plan is able to build sufficient membership in the new product (either by converting existing members to the new product model or attracting new members), it will demand greater pricing concessions to remain in the lowest tier. The hospital will then have to decide whether to participate.

Every market is different, and the response to these different products is a function of the local market. Diligence in maintaining current awareness regarding benefit designs and plans being introduced into the market will prevent the healthcare provider from being surprised by what ultimately evolves. Proactive strategy development will ensure that the organization is properly positioned for new products entering the local market.

CHAPTER 4

How Do I Negotiate Effective Contracts with Insurers?

This chapter looks at negotiation strategies and contract terms that are important to consumer-directed products

NEGOTIATION

Negotiation is a process whereby each party strives to enrich not only itself but also the other party to create a mutually beneficial relationship. Entering a negotiation with an "I must win–they must lose" mentality might serve the negotiator well for this one negotiation; however, if both parties are not enriched by the arrangement, the party that is disadvantaged will attempt to remedy the situation in subsequent negotiations or during the administration of the current arrangement. ▶

In the negotiation process, often several levels of terms are being negotiated at the same time. For example, negotiators might be trying to achieve organizational objectives (e.g., locking in a long-term contract, introducing a new product) or personal objectives (e.g., getting an annual bonus, completing the deal before vacation).

No matter what the agenda, the negotiator should be aware that the parties with whom he or she is negotiating usually do not have the final authority to conclude the transaction, despite what they might assert. It follows, then, that negotiators present proposals within the limits of their authority. Thus, to be an effective negotiator, you would present enough information to the participants on the other side to educate them on your position so that they can sell the ultimate deal to their superiors. Approaching negotiation from an educational viewpoint also often keeps personal conflicts from entering the process.

SOURCES OF POWER IN NEGOTIATION

No discussion of negotiation would be complete without a review of some of the key sources of power. A major factor influencing an organization's approach to negotiation is its use and perception of power. Power is often a matter of perception, and each party has more power than it realizes. The goal for a negotiator is to focus on the limitations on the other side's power rather than the limitations on his or her own power. Each party obtains its power from several sources, including acting consistently, being informed, fostering personal relationships, and being prepared.

Acting Consistently

Acting in a consistent manner is a significant source of power. The fact that the Saturn Corporation never negotiates its auto prices, for example, lends significant leverage to that company. A payer that consistently applies its pricing and product strategy can lend as much power to the organization as the strategy itself. Other examples include the following:

- The health plan that pays all physicians according to one fee schedule with no exceptions
- Health plans that have a definite approach to hospital pricing, both in methodology and rates, and are not willing to enter into contracts with those who want to deviate from their approach

Assign at least two people in the organization the responsibility of developing an ongoing relationship with two key people in the top four or five health plans in your market, whether or not you currently contract with these plans. This will ensure continuity of the relationship in the event that one person leaves the organization. At least once a quarter meet with the other party in a casual, social situation, if possible. Use this time to determine what the organization views to be important, what new products are in the planning and development stages, what it expects from you, and so forth. This information can help you assess the impact of the other party's plans on your relationship well before they are introduced. You might even develop a report card on the health plan's performance from your perspective and share it with the plan. The time to learn this information is not at the negotiating table, or worse, when the other party decides to terminate or significantly modify the relationship.

- Health systems that own multiple hospitals in a market and require health plans to contract with all of the system's hospitals or not contract with it at all
- The hospital or physician organization that has a true competitive advantage in the market and commands higher prices than the competition because it consistently applies its pricing strategy and does not disadvantage any major payer in the process

The best way for a negotiator to deal with these types of situations is to test the consistency argument by remembering that everything is negotiable and the stated position is not always the final position.

Being Informed

Information is power. Each party needs to take the time to know the other party's business as well as they know their own. Understanding the definition of terms, medical underwriting techniques, product pricing strategies, market positioning of products, and decision-making processes can provide valuable insight. For example, knowing how the party with whom you are negotiating is compensated and what their incentives are can be a source of power. You might be surprised to learn that a negotiator gets compensated on a point system for the contracts he or she negotiates, and thus certain terms are more important to him or her over others based on their point values.

Fostering Personal Relationships

The development of personal relationships between the parties is critical. Relationships facilitate the gathering of information and development of respect and trust between the parties. People are much more willing to work out an agreement when a relationship exists.

It is important to develop an ongoing relationship before sitting down to negotiate a contract. Once the negotiation process begins, each party's motivation becomes suspect, even to parties intent on creating a mutually beneficial relationship. If trust is established early in the relationship, it is easier to develop a win-win outcome.

Developing personal relationships helps the negotiator determine the individual needs of people in the other party. These needs are just as important to meet in a negotiation as those of the organization; however, rarely are they as obvious as the organizational objectives. For example, maybe a participant from the other party is looking for another position and is not interested in the long-term effect the contract will have. This kind of information is rarely learned over the negotiating table but can prove very valuable in developing a negotiating strategy.

Being Prepared

Successful negotiation begins with thorough preparation: Take all the time necessary to get to know the payer and the payer's needs. Develop an understanding of the strategic direction in which the payer is moving. Review all public data available on the payers. It is important to know as much about the payer's business as the payer does to position your organization to meet its needs while meeting your own. Preparation can be a significant source of power to those willing to invest the time and effort.

It is not possible to use good negotiation tactics without a good negotiation strategy. During the preparation phase, develop the strategy and include what tactics you will use and when and how you will use them.

CONTRACT TERMS

This section addresses the contract terms that are important to understand when dealing with not only the consumer-directed products to come but also the current products. This section should not be viewed as legal advice; the reader is encouraged to seek appropriate legal review before signing payer contracts.

Nonprice terms can be just as important as price terms in contracts. Be sure to give yourself enough time to fully negotiate these important terms. The effective negotiator is one who, among other things, informs the organization about how long it will take to develop an effective agreement. By preparing the organization for a long negotiation, the negotiator is not pressured into spending an inadequate amount of time on the important nonprice terms. (As with the factors listed above, the effective management of time can be a significant source of power for the negotiator.)

Definitions

The definition section of a contract is perhaps the most boring section but is also the most important. Take the time to read and understand the definitions in the contract. Remember

CONSIDER THIS

Treat the other party as customers or potential customers. Hospitals and healthcare organizations routinely survey their patients, physicians, and personnel to determine their satisfaction levels with the organization. These same hospitals rarely survey the payers. Surveying the payers is just as important because if their needs are not being met, there may be no patients to survey. The organization that routinely determines the needs of the health plan and meets those needs will be better positioned as a payer-friendly organization than the competition. This positioning can become a source of power in your negotiations.

that a lawyer's responsibility is to protect you from liability, not to protect you from a bad business deal.

The definitions in this section pertain to the *products that are included in the contract*. Be sure to understand, for example, whether the contract includes indemnity products that the insurer might manage. Is workers' compensation included? Are discount clubs that issue discount cards able to access your hospital? Often, the contracting party will take the position that all of its products are included unless specifically omitted from the contract.

NETWORK DESIGN. The providers in the health plan's network influence the amount of business that you can expect to receive. Thus, it is important to define the network and the pricing for the network in the contract. Changes to the network should result in changes to the prices in the contract because the network influences one of the key factors in establishing price: expected volume. Language should be put in the contract that prohibits leasing a part of a network. Say, for example, a large employer wants all of the area's hospitals to participate in the network except your hospital. This should not be permitted, as you are expecting the entire network to be offered to all potential customers.

Three potential approaches are available to determine the network/price relationship.

1. The health plan and hospital could agree that the rates allow the health plan to contract for a specific number of licensed beds within certain zip codes. This would permit the health plan to change its network but limit the number of hospitals with which it could contract.

2. The hospital and health plan could agree on a specific network, which, if changed by the health plan, would require renegotiation of rates or permit the hospital to terminate the contract.

3. The hospital and health plan could agree to networks and rate schedules associated with each network. This way the health plan could change its network, but the hospital would already have a predetermined rate established.

Whatever method is established, it is important that the contract specify the network hospitals for the rates that are being provided, if this is important in the price development to the hospital.

NETWORK ACCESS. An important consideration in leased preferred provider organization (PPO) contracts is when access to the network is permitted. Health plans that have their own network in a market have recently begun leasing networks to cover their out-of-network business. It works this way: Say Health Plan A has a network in your market, and you have not contracted with Health Plan A. You have contracted to be in Health Plan B's network, and Health Plan B is a leased PPO. A patient who is insured by Health Plan A is admitted to your hospital or comes to your physician office. The patient is out of network, so Health Plan A should pay you full billed charges less deductibles, coinsurance, or copayments. Health Plan A contracts with Health Plan B to lease B's network and uses Health Plan B's discount when patients are out of network. Health Plan A benefits by getting in-network rates when its member is actually out of network.

Most contracts that lease a health plan's network contain clauses that say it will use its best efforts to encourage the lessor's members to utilize network providers. Because Health Plan A does not include your organization in its network, I would consider Health Plan A to be in breach of this provision and should not be entitled to take Health Plan B's discounts. Further, when health plans use this leased discount, they are usually treating their member as being out of network and apply the higher coinsurance or copayments, and yet they are taking an in-network discount. This does not seem to be a fair representation to the member. Either your organization is in the network or it is not; the health plan should not be able to have it both ways.

Clear language in the contract will help you to disallow this kind of behavior on the part of an unscrupulous health plan. Thus, to prevent such behavior from health plans that can lease their network, you will need to include language in your contracts that prohibits leasing to a plan that has an established network in your market.

WHO IS LEASING THE NETWORK?

Many of the leading consumer-directed companies (e.g., Definity.com, Lumenous.com) lease existing networks rather than form their own. It is important that the hospital and physician know which companies are leasing which products. Thus, language should be included in each contract with health plans that lease their network requiring that the plans disclose on a periodic basis or through a posting on their web site which companies can currently lease the network. This way the hospital or provider can better track the amount of high-deductible plans through a particular contract and determine if rate adjustments are necessary.

The provider or hospital needs to begin collecting payment and bad debt data by benefit plan design. This process will add another administrative burden on the hospital, but it is important to have the necessary data that show the uncollectible amounts when negotiating new rates with the payer.

BENEFIT DESIGN. Benefit design is perhaps the most important element of the contract to consider as you evaluate the new consumer-driven products and their impact on your healthcare organization. Pricing negotiated by hospitals in contracts is often based on several factors, including anticipated volume, the ease of administration of the contract, and the amount being paid by the plan and the member. If any of these factors change, the nature of the agreement changes. For example, if the health plan introduces policies

that complicate the administration of the contract, an appropriate adjustment to the price is needed. Similarly, if the plan introduces health savings account products with high deductibles that the provider needs to collect, appropriate adjustment to the contract rates should be made to account for increased bad debt and cost of collection. Not making these adjustments to price results in increased risk to the provider.

Because plans are rapidly changing their benefit designs to meet the competition, it is strongly recommended that hospitals obtain the benefit designs being offered by each health plan with which the hospital contracts on at least an annual basis.

ENFORCING BENEFIT DESIGNS. As mentioned above in the Network Design section of this chapter, one of the important factors affecting the price that the provider charges the health plan is the volume the provider expects to receive. The primary driver in keeping patients within the health plan's network is its benefit design, specifically, the coinsurance requirement for out-of-network use and, in some cases, the amount of the out-of-pocket maximum for out-of-network use.

Typically in point-of-service (POS) and PPO products, these amounts are higher for out-of-network use. These benefit designs are only as good as their enforcement by the health plan.

With the emergence of provider-owned diagnostic centers, surgery centers, and hospitals comes the temptation by those not in network to "waive" the out-of-network copayment to patients in return for their use of the out-of-network facility. This creates legal difficulties for those out-of-network providers who do this; however, enforcement is almost nonexistent in most markets. The potential legal difficulties arise in three areas: insurance fraud, consumer fraud, and tortuous interference with a contract.

Insurance fraud. The following example illustrates the principle of insurance fraud. Say a patient has a health plan with a coinsurance requirement of 10 percent when in network and 30 percent when out of network. Assume the billed charge for the services received by the patient at the out-of-network facility is $10,000. The facility and the patient agree prior to the patient receiving services that the patient will only have to pay 10 percent (i.e., $1,000) rather than the 30 percent coinsurance that would normally be charged for out-of-network services. The facility bills the health plan the full $10,000 charge. However, the agreed-to price is really $8,000 because the facility is waiving the $2,000 difference between the 10 percent coinsurance and the 30 percent coinsurance. Thus, the facility should be billing the health plan $8,000, not $10,000; by billing the latter amount, insurance fraud is committed.

However, few state-elected insurance commissioners enforce this type of fraud against insurance companies because they cannot run for election on the platform, "I made you pay your full copayment!" From their perspective, the patient is not harmed, so there is no real problem. Even though this type of fraud charge is often not pursued, the organization has the ethical responsibility not to engage in this kind of practice.

The way to avoid this legal issue is for the facility to write a letter informing the health plan that it routinely waives coinsurance. Because the health plan has received notice, no fraud will take place. However, the health plan should advise the facility that it will be reducing the billed charges submitted for each bill by the amount of the waiver and calculating payment accordingly. Also, should the facility decide to reduce its charges to the patient further, it needs to notify the health plan or it will be committing insurance fraud.

Consumer fraud. Consider the same example of a patient who has a health plan with a coinsurance requirement of 10 percent when in network and 30 percent when out of network. Assume the billed charge for the services received by the patient at the out-of-network facility is $10,000. In this case, prior to receiving care the patient talks with the facility and is assured that "we will treat you as if you are in network and only charge you 10 percent coinsurance." Depending on the patient's subsequent actions, this may or may not be an example of consumer fraud.

If the patient were in network, he or she would have to pay 10 percent coinsurance, but that payment is based on a contracted rate, which is usually significantly lower than an out-of-network facility's billed charges. Thus, the patient, in most cases, would end up paying more by going out of network than by staying in network. For example, if the in-network facility contracted with the health plan to accept $5,000 to treat the patient for this procedure, the member would only have to pay $500, not the $1,000 he or she would have ended up paying to the out-of-network facility. The implied promise to the patient, however, was that his or her costs would be no higher than if he or she had gone to a network facility.

The way to avoid this legal issue is to waive the entire amount of the coinsurance. Thus, because the patient would be paying nothing, he or she could never pay more than would have been paid had he or she gone to a network facility.

Tortuous interference with a contract. The health plan has a contract with the employer and the employees/members. This contract requires that members pay a higher coinsurance for out-of-network use. By waiving the coinsurance or a portion of the coinsurance the facility is interfering with that contract and is subject to a civil claim.

With the advent of higher deductibles and coinsurance amounts patients will shop based on the best pricing arrangement they can get. In response, more facilities may begin to negotiate directly with patients to offer reductions in the amount of coinsurance required to be paid in return for getting their business. Thus, it is important that providers require health plans to enforce their benefit designs and that appropriate language to that effect be put in the contract.

If health plans are willing to permit tortuous interference with a contract, then in-network providers have to question the value of being in network. Why would an in-network provider not terminate its contract with a health plan that does not take aggressive action and just waive the coinsurance itself? In fact, the provider could even advertise that it does waive coinsurance. Certainly its financial return would be better.

Another approach that would demonstrate a health plan's commitment to keeping as much business in network as possible is to establish payment limits for out-of-network use. For example, the health plan may define the out-of-network benefit as 100 percent of the Medicare allowable amount less the copayment or coinsurance.

Finally, a health plan could not accept assignment for out-of-network services and pay the member directly. These two measures would discourage out-of-network providers from negotiating special arrangements with a potential patient to nullify the intent of the out-of-network benefit.

A question has emerged as to whether the calculation of when the deductible is met should be based on the contracted rate or the provider's billed charges. The prevailing consensus has been that the deductible should be based on the discounted rates in the contract similar to how the coinsurance is calculated. However, an argument can be made that because the contract does not begin providing coverage until the deductible has been met, billed charges should be used. The agreed-to approach should be clarified in the contract.

Changes that Affect the Nature of the Agreement

Unilateral changes to the contract should not be permitted unless notice is given and an opportunity is provided to evaluate the impact of the proposed change and renegotiate if necessary or terminate the contract prior to the implementation of the change. Such language should, at a minimum, apply to changes to the following:

- *Payment rates.* Some contracts do not include rate schedules but make reference to them. For example, a health plan might reference its national lab fee schedule and apply the same rate to the hospital outpatient lab services. When this

CONSIDER THIS

Include in your contract language the stipulation that the health plan is required to enforce its benefit designs. For cases in which you learn that waiving of coinsurance has occurred, report it to the plan and require the plan to follow up. One health plan sent the following letter to violators as a result of such contract language:

Dear_____:

According to our records your facility, _____, has been accepting Health Plan A Inc. ("HPA") Members. This letter is to advise you that we do not authorize, and expressly oppose, any program by which a nonparticipating provider such as your facility attempts to attract our Members (whether full-insured or covered through self-insured employers) by offering to waive the copayments, coinsurance, or deductibles under their applicable benefit plan.

Such arrangements undermine the benefit plan by eliminating the incentives created to encourage Members to choose to receive care within their network and discourage overutilization of services. Such schemes have long been illegal under the federal antikickback laws when used in connection with federally funded programs such as Medicaid and Medicare.

Such arrangements may also constitute insurance fraud in violation of federal law (see 18 U.S.C. § 1347) because the claim submitted by the provider misrepresents the provider's actual charge, with the intent that the insurer or employer detrimentally relies on that misrepresentation. Specifically, if the submitted charge is $1,000, and the Member's benefit plan provides for 30% coinsurance, but the provider waives the $300 coinsurance, then the provider's true billed charge is $700 and not the $1,000 submitted to the health carrier.

Finally, such arrangements may also constitute wrongful interference with HPA's business relationships with its employer customers and with its Members. Under our Members' benefit plans, the Members are specifically obligated to pay for any and all coinsurance and copayment amounts. The practice of waiving coinsurance directly interferes with the contract HPA has executed with its customers, and HPA is contractually obligated to enforce such contracts.

HPA takes the issue of routine waivers of copayments, coinsurance, and deductibles seriously. We trust that your facility will not engage in any such arrangements involving HPA Members now that our position has been made clear to you, and that you will immediately cease and desist from any such arrangements should they currently be in effect.

We request a written acknowledgment from you that your facility is in compliance with this letter. Failure to voluntarily comply will necessitate that HPA avail itself of all legal remedies to prevent continued waiver of copayments, coinsurance, and/or deductibles.

Sincerely,

Chief Executive Officer

happens it is important that the fee schedule be attached to the contract and that changes to it not be permitted without prior approval of the provider.

- *Bundling or grouping of procedures*. Health plans use bundling software that combines services into one payment code. This software is frequently updated and often results in a different payment from the contracted rate. Some contracts contain language indicating that the provider will follow the bundling methodology established by the health plan or consistent with industry standards. By agreeing to this the provider is allowing the payer to change the methodology used and affect the payment rates agreed to in the contract. The health plan should be required to notify the provider prior to making changes in the bundling methodology so that the provider can assess the impact of these changes. The provider and payer should also agree that if changes result in different payment from the contracted rated, rates will be adjusted to ensure that the provider receives the overall agreed-to rate.

- *Administrative procedures*. To ensure that changes that conflict with the intent of the contract are not implemented, language should be included in contracts similar to the following:

  Manuals serve an administrative purpose in implementing the relationship between the parties. It is not the mutual intent of the parties that any term of the manuals will contradict, modify, or otherwise affect the terms of the Contract. In the event of a conflict or inconsistency between this Contract and any exhibit, attachment, plan program, policy, manual, or any other document affecting this Contract, the provisions of this Contract shall control.

- *The network of hospital providers*. One of the factors contributing to the rates charged by the providers is the extent to which competing providers are in the payers' network. This is particularly true for hospitals. The nature of the agreement would change if the health plan were to add hospitals to the network. No longer could the hospital assume that it would receive the volume it planned on receiving if a competing hospital were added. Thus, the hospital would want to charge the payer more because there is now more competition for the payer's patients. At a minimum a provider should receive notice when new providers are added to the network. Ideally the hospital should retain the right to negotiate new rates if the network changes.

- *Benefit designs.* Because benefit designs affect total payment to be received, providers should, at a minimum, set up procedures to track bad debt by plan design. This practice puts them in a better position to quantify the impact of high-deductible plans on their bad debt. If adjustments to rates were not made prospectively to account for these new benefit designs, the provider, by having this data, will be in a better position to negotiate rate improvements retrospectively.

TIERED HOSPITAL COINSURANCE/ COPAYMENT AMOUNTS.

Health plans that place hospitals or physicians in tiers are in effect creating small networks within a network. Typically health plans that tier hospitals or physicians retain the contracted rate with the provider and change the benefit design by requiring higher copayments for the patient.

Hospitals and physicians should consider including language in their contracts that does not permit placing providers in different tiers without renegotiating the rates in place. Because one of the key components to rate establishment is anticipated volume, any change that directs business away from the provider affects that anticipated volume. As such, whenever changes of this kind are made, rates needs to be reevaluated and modified as necessary. The provider must initiate these discussions as soon as they learn about changes affecting volume, or they will not get the volume on which the rates were predicated.

Providers concerned about a tiered benefit design need to consider contract language that prohibits a health plan from sending members (either directly or indirectly) to specific providers or away from specific providers in the network without notifying the provider and negotiating an appropriate rate adjustment or allowing the provider to terminate the agreement.

RIGHT TO MEMBER-LEVEL ACCESS.

One of the critical factors necessary for a consumer-directed health plan to be effective is member education. Health plans adopting consumer-directed products are attempting to make it easy for their members to obtain information on price and quality to help them make decisions about which providers to use.

It is important that the provider knows what information is being given to the health plan members for at least two reasons. First, patients or potential patients are likely to contact the provider with questions about the information they are receiving. The provider needs to know the same information and how it was derived to be in a better position to explain it. Second, a lot of misinformation is available to patients. A health plan may be using old data, adjusting it in a unique manner, or simply misrepresenting it. The provider should be able to correct the data being presented or at least to offer an explanation to those searching the information.

Thus, the provider should require in the contract with the health plan that, at a minimum, the health plan will allow the provider access to the health plan's web site with a dummy sign-on. This way the provider can stay current with the information being made available to members of the plan. Ideally, the provider should be able to post comments or a link to comments that the provider feels the member should consider when reviewing the data on the health plan's web site.

Members are often looking for quick and easy answers to their questions. Those on the provider side realize that this is usually not possible and that data can be manipulated to suit any purpose. Until there is a standard approach to how to measure quality and what information is important and what is not, providers need to at least be aware of what is being made available to members in health plans with which they contract. This may influence whether a provider chooses to contract with a plan or the rates at which the provider will contract. If the information being presented influences patients to choose specific providers over others to your detriment, then you need to reconsider your pricing algorithm with the payer.

BEING LISTED IN THE PROVIDER DIRECTORY. In many markets freestanding outpatient diagnostic centers and surgery centers are rapidly developing as formidable competitors with hospitals. Hospitals are often only listed in the health plan's provider directory or on the health plan's web site under the "Hospital" category. When a member searches the web site or provider directory for in-network providers of outpatient surgery or imaging, they are directed to a listing of the freestanding centers, placing the hospitals at a disadvantage.

Hospitals need to ensure that they are listed in all of the areas of the provider directory or web site where health plan members might look to determine who is in network, or the volume that was anticipated in the contract might not materialize.

PRICING STRATEGY. It is important to note that most high-deductible plans are usually offered on the health insurer's PPO or POS platform because these have fewer restrictions from a regulatory point of view than an HMO product has. As a hospital develops its pricing strategy regarding the plans with which it wants to participate, the platform becomes an important element. For example, in years past, HMO products have received the best rates from providers; low or no copayments, coinsurance, or deductibles were involved; and members were restricted to using the network offered. Hospitals and physicians knew they would get paid by the health plan and not have to engage in collection activities. They also could count on the HMO to direct volume to network providers. Preferred provider organizations and point-of-service products usually paid

more to hospitals and physicians because they had to collect a portion of the payment and out-of-network use was permitted.

Today, many health plans want to develop one rate schedule for all products, explaining that this will ease their administration and lower costs to their customers. Often they want to blend the existing fee schedules using a weighted average approach, thereby paying the hospitals the same aggregate amount that was paid in the past. By accepting this approach of one fee schedule the hospital is assuming that the mix of business between the HMO and PPO/POS products will remain the same. Because most high-deductible plans are usually offered on the health insurer's PPO or POS platform, if these products grow in your market, this blending approach will result in lower payments to the hospital over time than the current multiple-rate approach.

Further, in many states, high-deductible plans are not permitted on HMO products. This will result in HMO products being priced higher in the market than PPO/POS products, the direct opposite of the historical relationship between the two products. In those states growth will probably occur in PPO/POS products simply because of the cost difference for employers. Thus, the product mix and future product growth should be considered as the party that is establishing prices does so for these new consumer-directed products.

TIMING FOR COLLECTING THE DEDUCTIBLE OR COINSURANCE. It

may seem obvious to the hospital or physician that the deductible or coinsurance can be collected prior to providing nonemergent services. However, some health plans have recently taken the position that the deductible and/or coinsurance cannot be collected at the time of service because the final charge for the service is unknown. The health plan cannot tell a provider who calls to learn the balance of the unmet deductible what that balance is with certainty because billing that would affect the balance may be processed later. Thus, the health plan asserts that the provider must wait until it receives the remittance advice from the health plan to determine the amount to collect from the patient. However, for a patient with a $5,000 deductible, the hospital may be reluctant to perform the procedure without an up-front deposit.

To avoid this problem, language should be included in the contract to permit up-front payment of the deductible by the patient in a nonemergent situation with the commitment by the hospital to rebate any overpayment within a certain number of days after determining that an overpayment has been made.

A similar situation exists for coinsurance. Often the hospital does not know what the contracted rate will be until after the service is provided. Hospitals need to develop a better system to determine a patient's bill upon discharge, similar to that of a hotel. With that type of billing system, the hospital could run the patient's credit card upon admission and bill the patient his or her coinsurance upon discharge. Hospitals that are able to figure out such a process are likely to reduce their collection problems and bad debt experience.

Liability

An attorney should review your contracts before they are executed to protect the hospital from liability. Health plans recently have been putting language in contracts that attempts to shift liability for all decisions regarding a patient's care to the provider. The hospital or provider should attempt to include language whereby the health plan acknowledges that decisions regarding what services are covered and how the health plan benefit is designed influences whether patients follow their physician's advice or recommended course of treatment. With higher deductibles and copayments patients may chose not to follow the recommended course of treatment and then later sue the doctor or hospital for not providing it. The health plans that are offering these types of plans should acknowledge that their products do influence patients' decisions.

Favored Nations

Favored nations is a provision requiring the provider to give the payer the best price. In the event that the provider gives a better rate to another payer, the provider is also required to give it to the payer with the contract containing the favored-nations provision. Two considerations are worth noting regarding favored-nations clauses.

First, you must determine when to apply a favored-nations provision. This determination is simple when all of an organization's contracts are under the same basic payment structure (e.g., all are per diem, all are based on a discount off of charges). However, how do you compare prices

when all of the contracts are based on different pricing schemes (e.g., some are based on a discount off of charges, some are per diem, some are case rates)? For example, to determine a comparable per diem, do you convert a case rate to a per diem by dividing the case rate by the average length of stay of the payer that has the favored-nations provision, or by the length of stay of the payer with the case rate? Or do you convert all contracts to discount off of charges and compare the discount percentages? Is it fair to compare different pricing structures when each has its unique incentives and different degrees of risk? Unless these questions are addressed when the contract is being negotiated and a clear agreement is reached, potential conflicts may arise over these issues in the future.

Second, for those who negotiate physician fees, favored nations may be a valuable contract term to include. Most health plans that pay on a fee-for-service basis use the resource-based relative value system that Medicare uses as well as one fee schedule per product for all physicians in the same specialty. This is the perfect situation in which to ask for a favored-nations provision whereby the health plan will pay you its best rate for the physicians in your specialty. Because the health plan is paying everyone the same, it should be willing to do that. If it is unwilling to include this provision in the contract, the physician needs to probe further to ensure that he or she is getting the best rate.

NEGOTIATION TIPS

To conclude this chapter we review a few key negotiation tips that should result in improved contracts for those choosing to use them.

Develop a Checklist

Develop a checklist of important provisions that you want to see in a contract. Then test every contract against that checklist. Most payers want to use their contract form. If you spend your time editing their contract you might forget some key points that you want included. By using a checklist you can make certain that you have not omitted an important provision. A sample checklist is contained in the appendix, "Sample Payer Contract Checklist: ABC Health Plan," at the end of the book. It can serve as a starting point for developing a checklist that specifically meets your organization's needs.

Use a Team

Payer contracts can be very complicated and involve several departments within the organization. Do not hesitate to use a team of people to help you prepare for the negotiation. Teams offer many advantages, including the following:

- Better buy-in to the ultimate outcome of the negotiation by the organization
- Increased ability to listen and hear the other side's needs and views
- Decreased likelihood of making a mistake
- Better understanding of the issues because more experts contribute to the process
- Increased ability to delegate and divide the work so it can be done in a more timely and thorough manner
- Better continuity should there be turnover within the organization
- An opportunity to train future negotiators

The major disadvantage of using teams is that significantly more coordination is required among team members. This often lengthens the negotiation process.

The mix of talent, interpersonal skills, and expertise on the team is critical. In addition, the level of organizational leadership represented on the team sends an important signal to the other party regarding the significance attached to the particular negotiation.

Not all team members need to attend each negotiation session. However, each should be involved in setting the objectives, negotiating strategy, and negotiating parameters when specific questions arise involving their area of expertise and when the need arises to modify the negotiation strategy.

Once a team is in place it is important to select a spokesperson. This individual will direct the negotiations of the team. Other members of the team should not speak during the negotiation session unless directed by the spokesperson. This is perhaps the most difficult aspect of teams for the team members themselves to accept: all of the members are bright, talented people in their areas of expertise, and all will have a desire to contribute. However, they must be willing to subject themselves to the use of a spokesperson to ensure that one view is presented, it is consistent, and there is team agreement in the approach. To do otherwise weakens the team.

Set Expectations High and Be the First to Suggest Major Terms

Set high expectations that are justified based on your objectives and supported with data (including the other party's data when available). Those who set high and reasonable targets and stick to them often get what they want out of a contract.

Be the first to suggest major terms rather than reacting to others' suggestions. It is important to remember that negotiation has a tendency to play on personal aspirations, as in the following example.

An HMO comes to a healthcare organization requesting a per diem proposal. The organization knows that it can provide the service for a minimum of $800 per day but would like to get at least $1,200 per day. The hospital asks the health plan what its pricing expectations are, and the health plan submits its desired pricing of $600 per day. The natural reaction is for the negotiator of the healthcare organization to immediately begin to move his or her expectation toward the lower end of the range.

In essence the negotiator begins to negotiate with himself or herself, assuming that the health plan will never accept the higher proposal. If, however, the provider organization proposes a higher amount first, say $1,500 per day, the targets tend to move toward the higher amount. Although this approach may seem counterintuitive initially, placing your offer on the table first will achieve results closer to your desired outcome than will waiting and responding to someone else's offer. Setting your expectations high should obviate the fear of "leaving something on the table," or not getting the best deal. This is a common phrase in the negotiation arena.

Remember that you will never know whether your proposal will be accepted if you do not ask. Do not worry that something might be left on the table. Take the previous example; if you accept the $600 offer without any negotiation, the payer is led to believe that it could have gone lower, say $500. Hence you would have left $100 on the table. Be satisfied with the targets that you set.

Never Accept the First Offer

Never accept the first offer that is made, even if it is acceptable to your organization. Both parties need to feel that the results are good for both sides. If one party accepts the other's initial offer, most often the feeling by the party making the offer is that something was left on the table. In long-term relationships, maintaining the relationship is as important as the ultimate arrangement.

Use an Attorney Whose Motto Is "Can Do"

When selecting an attorney to assist in your contract negotiations, choose one who will listen to your objectives and help fashion a proposal to meet the organization's business needs while pointing out legal risks. Remember that the ultimate business deal is the responsibility of the provider, not the attorney. The attorney's role is to protect the organization from unnecessary liability, not from a bad business deal.

Attorneys are trained to conduct proceedings in the adversarial mode and thus should not be the party conducting the negotiations because they are less inclined to look for win-win solutions. They should review the contract during the preparation for negotiations, pointing out areas of liability. The actual negotiations should be conducted by someone very familiar with the operations necessary to implement the contract.

Keep It Simple

Any conditions to which you agree must be administered by the organization, so seek simplicity: the terms of the contract must be able to be properly administered by the health plan. The goal should be that almost all claims that are submitted are automatically paid according to the contract, thereby avoiding manual intervention and potential misinterpretation of the contract.

Hospitals should run sample claims through the health plans' system to ensure that they will be paid properly and that what was negotiated can actually be administered.

Document Everything

Documentation is very important throughout the negotiation process. Minutes should be kept of every negotiating session. Confirm in writing to the other party those items on which there is basic agreement as well as those issues that are still outstanding. This documentation can prove invaluable should one or more of the parties involved in the actual negotiation leave their respective organization. How the agreement was reached and the intent of the parties is easier to determine if minutes of the negotiating sessions are available.

Prepare

We began this chapter talking about preparation, and we end it with the same message. The 80/20 rule applies when negotiating contracts: 80 percent of the time related to negotiating a contract should be devoted to preparing for the negotiation and 20 percent to the actual negotiation. It is important that the negotiating team know as much about the other side's business as that business's negotiators do, including the other side's business goals and product strategies. Take the time to analyze the available data to fully understand the risks being assumed. These risks will have a major impact on the contracting strategy that is adopted.

Once in the negotiation, 80 percent of the time spent should be on the major issues in the contract. If the major issues cannot be resolved, there is no need to worry about the minor ones. You can focus the discussion on those major issues by creating an agenda for each meeting and sticking to it.

To achieve maximum results in your negotiations, set your expectations high; be the first to offer major terms; and remember, you never know whether or not something is acceptable to the other party unless you ask.

CHAPTER 5

Where Will Consumer-Directed Care Take Us?

Where is the trend of demanding discounts without delivering volume likely to lead?

A significant movement is underway challenging whether not-for-profit organizations deserve their tax-exemption status. The issue has been framed as one relating to hospitals' approaches to dealing with charges and collections from the uninsured. Central to the challenge is the fact that hospitals often give large discounts to payers but charge the uninsured patient the full billed charges. Many believe that this is unfair and that the uninsured are bearing a disproportionate share of the overall reimbursement to hospitals. Regardless of your position on the issue, it is fair to say that many hospitals have responded ▶

by putting in place discount arrangements based on the ability of patients to pay.

Workers' compensation payers have been challenging hospitals' charge structures as well. Often they bring suit demanding that hospitals produce their commercial contracts during the discovery process and claim that they should be entitled to discounts similar to those offered to commercial health plans, which provide significantly more business to the organization. Hospitals many times will refuse to produce their contracts and often end up settling for a large discount from these companies.

What is lost in these initiatives is that hospitals have long given discounts in return for volume from payers. The benefit designs and the restrictive networks that were in place usually drove this volume to the hospital. The uninsured patient who could have afforded to purchase health insurance but opted not to and who is now facing a large health insurance bill feels that he or she is being treated unfairly. Public sympathy appears to be with this individual (despite the fact that the patient chose not to purchase health insurance when he or she could have done so). The workers' compensation

carrier that delivers limited business to the hospital also feels entitled to a discount.

THE FUTURE AND CONSUMER-DIRECTED PRODUCTS

Assume that the patient has chosen the consumer-directed product and is now experiencing price transparency. A question one might ask is, Where is the trend of demanding discounts without delivering volume likely to lead? I believe that at least three outcomes are possible: a return to billed charges with very minimal discounts based on significant volume, rates based on a percentage of Medicare, or a national health plan.

Back to the Future: A Return to Billed Charges

The underlying premise for hospitals discounting their prices was that payers would drive business to the hospital through narrow networks and/or benefit designs in return for discounts. This was developed during a time when many markets had a surplus capacity of beds. Today, many of the bed surpluses have been eliminated because hospitals have converted this bed space to other uses. In addition, many health plans have moved away from narrow network products in favor of broad networks in response to their customers' wishes.

Hospitals need to reevaluate whether they should be discounting to payers. Hospitals have to ask if value is being received for the discount being offered. Further, many hospitals are paid based on per diem or case rates. By accepting this payment methodology the hospital is assuming a degree of risk. During times of excess capacity and narrow networks this degree of risk was deemed to be acceptable to the hospital. Hospitals need to ask whether it is still acceptable today. A possible scenario to emerge might consist of the following traits:

1. Hospitals recognize that they are no longer getting value for the discounts being offered. With all of the outside pressures on the complex nature of hospital pricing and the loss of value for discounting, hospitals might decide to restructure their pricing methods.
2. With the increased transparency of charges, hospitals will have access to competitors' prices.
3. Hospitals restructure their charges to be competitive and yield the desired net income return.

4. Hospitals terminate their existing contracts and implement the new pricing structure under which all payers will function. Hospitals may offer a modest (say, 5 percent) discount to the largest payer or two in their market in recognition of the volume they deliver, although that would not be required.

The end result is that hospital charges in most markets would be reduced, but billed charges would form the basis for payment. Further, hospitals would likely, over time, begin to function as a true oligopoly with charges of all hospitals in the market moving to be very close to each other. Under this scenario, these charges will approximate those of the highest-charge hospital in the market. Health plans will then compete on the basis of the value that they provide the purchaser, with hospital pricing no longer part of the equation.

Commercial Rates as a Percentage of Medicare

Another possible scenario is that insurance companies will move to products that provide a schedule of benefits and compensate all providers based on a percentage of Medicare allowances. Such a benefit design would allow the provider to balance bill the patient for the difference between the organization's billed charges and the scheduled rates. For example, inpatient cases might be paid at 120 percent of Medicare's rates. The patients then would be able to shop this rate and purchase from the hospital that provides them the best quality for the amount they have to spend.

National Health Plan

The provider community has long opposed national health insurance; however, recently some provider groups have begun calling for such a plan. With the uninsured approaching 46 million and the underinsured adding considerably more people with unmet healthcare needs, a potential scenario is a national health plan of some kind. A national health insurance plan would need to include the existing insurance structures in some form given their economic and political clout.

Health Plan Considerations

Over the short term, health plans can implement these consumer-driven products in an effort to engage the patient in his or her healthcare purchase decisions. This approach will make patients aware of price and could control utilization of some

lower-cost services, but not the high-cost services, which drive the majority of cost in the healthcare delivery system.

A long-term strategy that is beginning to gain some favor is pay for performance (P4P). Many different models are emerging that are designed to address the higher-cost services. While these models focus attention on areas that can simultaneously affect cost and quality, it is too early to determine whether this approach will be successful. For those interested in the latest P4P models for health plans, hospitals, and physicians, the reader can visit the Leapfrog Group's Incentive and Reward Compendium found at http://ir.leapfroggroup.org /compendium/.

NEED TO DEVELOP A PAYER STRATEGIC PLAN

Whatever model ultimately emerges, it is safe to say that providers need to remain vigilant as to the developments in benefit designs and develop proactive strategies to position their organizations for the future. In so doing, organizations need to have a written payer strategic plan that should include the following:

1. The type of relationship you want with each plan
   - Plans with which you just contract
   - Plans you want to see develop in your market
2. A consistent pricing strategy
   - Criteria relating to rates
     - Plan designs
     - Volume
     - Desire to see the plan grow
   - Criteria relating to when you will take risk and the type of risk you are willing to take
3. A product strategy
   - Will you selectively contract products from a payer?
   - Will you only contract all products or no products?
   - Which consumer-directed products meet your objectives?
   - Which benefit designs support your objectives?

In fashioning the payer strategic plan the key question that needs to be carefully addressed by the organization is whether the organization has a *real* competitive advantage—one that will drive enough patients to pay more to utilize your facility and allow your organization to grow and prosper in this new environment. If the answer to this question is that you do not have a real competitive advantage, then I suggest that developing one be your first step, or your organization's services will merely be viewed as a commodity.

Consumer-driven healthcare will place different pressures not only on hospitals but also on physicians. As you consider what is best for your organization in your market, remember the needs of the physicians in that market. A well-designed strategy can only be well designed if it considers the needs of the physicians in the market and attempts to address those needs as well.

A FINAL THOUGHT

As consumer-directed products succeed in attaining price transparency among hospitals, teaching hospitals and those hospitals that care for a disproportionate amount of uninsured patients will become vulnerable. Today, payers recognize the need to pay these organizations more to meet society's obligation to educate future healthcare providers and care for those who cannot afford to pay for it. As a result they tend to pay the organizations more. Price transparency will change this model to one in which the patient has to pay more. It is likely that the patient will let price drive his or her selection process. Who will assume the role of paying for education and indigent care? Absent a thoughtful approach to these issues, it is possible that teaching hospitals and those with a greater portion of indigent care will have to restructure themselves to compete, possibly changing their fundamental mission and becoming community hospitals in order to survive. This unintended consequence of price transparency may result in a significant price to society and should be addressed now, rather than when the ultimate crisis emerges.

Sample Payer Contract Checklist: ABC Health Plan

Agreement Sections (Bolded provisions are those most important.)	High Preference	HMO/PPO
General Provisions		
Main body of the contract: It is recommended that the main body of the contract define the general terms governing the relationship. An appendix should be developed that governs the payment relationship. This structure makes the contract easier to use, particularly where different payment arrangements exist for different Payer products (e.g., PPO, POS, HMO, Medicare+Choice HMO, worker's compensation, managed indemnity). **It is important to clarify that the appendix governs in the event of a conflict.**		
Does the contract limit volume of services? (e.g., geography, ancillary services)	No	
Is the hospital or health system the primary or exclusive entity? • Are the major competitors excluded?	Yes	
Entities included: All system hospitals, home health/durable medical equipment, lab, radiology, and hospice?	Yes	

Note: This sample contract is not intended to serve as legal advice. Please consult an attorney prior to executing a payer contract.

Agreement Sections (Bolded provisions are those most important.)	High Preference	HMO/ PPO
Definitions		
"Clean Claim"—A suggested definition of a clean claim is, "A claim is deemed to be clean if Provider has not received written notice to the contrary from Plan or Payer within ___ days of receipt of the claim." As an alternative the Medicare+Choice (M+C) definition should be used: A "clean" claim is a claim that has no defect of impropriety, including lack of required substantiating documentation for noncontracting suppliers and providers, or particular circumstances requiring special treatment that prevents timely payment from being made on the claim [Section 1842 (c)(2)(B) of the Social Security Act]. A claim is clean even though the Medicare+Choice organization (M+CO) refers it to a medical specialist within the M+CO for examination. If additional substantiating documentation (e.g., medical record, encounter data) involves a source outside the M+CO, the claim is not considered "clean." Reference the clean claim definition in an attachment, requiring each box of an HCFA-1500 and UB-92 to be identified. If a claim is denied as not being clean, the reason for it not being clean should be clearly specified.	Yes	
Medically necessary services should be defined as healthcare services that a reasonably prudent physician would deem necessary for the diagnosis or treatment of illness or injury or to improve the functioning of a malformed body member.	Yes	
Are key terms clearly defined and acceptable?		
"Covered services"—Is it clear that Hospital can bill the patient for services deemed not to be covered services?	Yes	
"Member or insured"	Yes	
"Utilization review"—Are guidelines attached?	Yes	
"Emergency services" or "Emergency"	Yes	
Is there a clear definition of Plan and Payer (if Plan has arrangements allowing other payers to access Plan's network)? • Are discount clubs excluded?	Yes	
Is there a clear definition of the products covered under the agreement, including network rentals?	Yes	
A clear definition of the network should be included. Modification of the network should permit Hospital to renegotiate the rates based on the new network and affect the expected volume or terminate.	Yes	
Is it clear that health plans with networks in the market cannot lease the network for out-of-network services?	Yes	

Agreement Sections (Bolded provisions are those most important.)	High Preference	HMO/ PPO
Plan Obligations		
Are Payer policies incorporated by reference or attached? Consider the following language: **"Payer Organization represents that copies of all policies, procedures, plans, programs, agreements, manuals, and any other documents (collectively, the 'Policies') which describe the obligations of Provider pursuant to the Principal Agreement have been disclosed to Provider and are listed in Exhibit B. Except as provided below, Payer Organization may amend the Policies by providing not less than sixty (60) days prior written notice ('Amendment Notice') to Provider. If Provider objects to any such amendment, it shall notify Payer Organization within thirty (30) days after its receipt of the Amendment Notice, specifying in detail the basis for its objections. The parties shall negotiate in good faith to resolve their dispute. In the event the dispute cannot be resolved, Provider may notify Payer Organization of its intention to terminate the Agreement as of the date preceding the effective date of the amendment."**	Attached	
If by reference, are they provided?	Yes	
Does contract state, "Manuals serve an administrative purpose in implementing the relationship between the parties. It is not the mutual intent of the parties that any term of the manuals will contradict, modify, or otherwise affect the terms of the contract. In the event of a conflict or inconsistency between this Contract and any exhibit, attachment, plan program, policy, manual, or any other document affecting this Contract, the provisions of this Contract shall control."?	Yes	
Can Hospital terminate Payer for cause (late payments) from the Payer agreement yet keep the agreement intact with the other payers?	Yes	
Does Plan limit its audit capability to no more than one year?	Yes	
Does Plan retain the right to carve out future services and contract separately for them (e.g., mental health, vision care)? **• If yes, does Hospital retain either a right to participate in carve-outs or right of first refusal to retain the business?**	No Yes	
Are admission requirements clearly defined?	Yes	
Can Hospital terminate agreement within 30 days if disagreements on policy/ procedure changes cannot be resolved?	Yes	
Must Payer notify Hospital in writing of any new plans/payers joining the agreement?	Yes	
The patient-channeling mechanism is clearly defined (e.g., copayment differential of at least 20%, out-of-pocket maximum only applies to in-network services, the network will be limited to the following hospitals...)	Yes	
Are network provider directories provided annually or online?	Yes	

Agreement Sections (Bolded provisions are those most important.)	High Preference	HMO/ PPO
Plan Obligations (continued)		
Are notices sent for incoming and outgoing network providers?	Yes	
Are all plan payers listed in agreement and updated as changes occur?	Yes	
Plan agrees to give Hospital at least 60 days' notice before new or revised benefit plans are implemented to which this contract applies [as copayment amounts may change, thereby increasing provider liability, or other incentives redirecting patients to other providers may occur] and give Hospital the option to terminate or renegotiate.	Yes	
Can Hospital opt out of new plans added to the Payer agreement after the agreement is first signed?	Yes	
Are all participating hospitals listed in the agreement?	Yes	
Does Plan provide Hospital with physician-specific customer satisfaction and quality information reports and data for analysis to assist with medical management?	Yes	
Plan agrees to designate a claims contact person with authority to resolve claims issues.	Yes	
Plan agrees not to discriminate in its provider directory or other marketing materials or in its benefit designs in any way as to disadvantage the provider from being selected to provide services.	Yes	
Will Payer provide a dummy ID to its web site to permit monitoring by Hospital of the information being provided to members?	Yes	
Does Payer guarantee payment? Consider the following language: "Payer Organization shall be primarily obligated to reimburse Provider for services rendered to Members pursuant to the Principal Agreement. If Payer Organization disclaims any obligation to pay Provider for services rendered to Members, Payer Organization shall, for each Payer, either: • obtain a guaranty, in the form attached hereto as Exhibit D, from each Payer who will be responsible to pay Provider for services; or • provide evidence satisfactory to Provider that Provider is a third-party beneficiary of Payer Organization's agreement with Payer or will otherwise have standing to enforce Payer's obligations to pay for services rendered to Provider."	Yes	
If a PPO contract, "Provider reserves the right to bill Members for any services for which a Payer fails to make payment, provided, however, that if Payer Organization provides satisfactory evidence to Provider that such billing is prohibited by law, Provider shall not bill the Member."	Yes	
If a PPO contract, Payer must provide a payer resolution process. If documented and trended issues exist, Payer has 120 calendar days to resolve the issue(s) with payer. If the issue(s) are not resolved, Payer must terminate the payer.	Yes	
Is Payer required to identify the network and payer leasing the network on all member ID cards, explanations of benefits, and remittances?	Yes	

Agreement Sections (Bolded provisions are those most important.)	High Preference	HMO/ PPO
Plan Obligations *(continued)*		
Is silent PPO language in the agreement? For example, "Network shall not sell contracted rates or discount information to clients, brokers, other insurance plans, employers, members, or individuals retroactively from the date services were provided by PSO Participating Providers."	Yes	
Are payers barred from picking the lowest rate for each service from various plan contracts?	Yes	
Hospital Obligations		
Is "standard of care" language avoided or softened via "endeavor to provide at prevailing quality in the community" or "at same standard as peers"?	Yes	
Is the timely filing period defined to begin when the hospital knew the patient was covered by the health plan?	Yes	
In other than discount-off-of-charge arrangements, payers should not be able to request a hospital itemized bill.		
Is it Hospital's responsibility to subcontract for services not provided?	Yes	
Can Hospital transfer Members at its own discretion?	Yes	
Is there an antidisparagement clause?	No	
Are certain services required to be provided?	Yes	
Do Hospital and Payer agree to meet monthly to review and resolve outstanding issues?	Yes	
Indemnification		
Is it specifically stated that each party is liable for its own wrongs?	Yes	
Does the contract contain a "hold harmless" clause? If included, it should be reviewed by legal counsel and be mutual.	No	
Are Provider's legal and patient obligations limited to a 90-day maximum continuation of care if Plan becomes insolvent?	Yes	
Grievance Procedures and Arbitration		
There is a clearly defined dispute resolution procedure. Recommend the party with the concern submit it in writing to the other party. There must be a 30-day period from receipt of the issue for the steering committee (or other defined group) to meet and resolve the issue. If they are unable to resolve it, the CEOs of the organizations will have 30 days to resolve it. If resolution is not completed and no agreement is made to extend this 30-day period, the issue will proceed to binding arbitration.	Yes	
Are there rights of appeal that involve outside agencies (utilization review, etc.)?	Yes	
Are appeal rights specified in the contract? For each payer?	Yes	

Agreement Sections (Bolded provisions are those most important.)	High Preference	HMO/ PPO
Grievance Procedures and Arbitration *(continued)*		
If the agreement is long term, is there a mechanism for handling unanticipated changes (e.g., new services added by provider, new biogenetically engineered drugs). Suggestion: The unanticipated change is written and forwarded to the other party. The steering committee (or designated group) has 60 days to resolve. If unresolved, the CEOs meet and have 30 days to resolve, then binding arbitration takes place. The agreement should contain some statement of intent regarding how these issues should be handled (e.g., for new services added, Hospital agrees to charge Plan its incremental costs + 10% to implement these services as verified by the hospital's auditor, or new services will be paid at 80% of billed charges until there is an agreement on rates).	Yes	
Are prompt pay issues excluded from arbitration?	Yes	
Continuation of Care		
Are Provider's obligations limited to providing care for the remainder of the inpatient treatment, or 90 days, whichever is less, if the contract ends?	Yes	
Is postcontract care based on Provider's usual and customary charges?	Yes	
Compensation		
Are payments made within 30 calendar days of submission of claims ?	Yes	
Is Payer penalized by reverting to billed charges if late in making payments?	Yes	
Is the time limit for submission of claims at least 180 days? Is timely filing measured from the date of service or 180 days from the date Provider is informed of coverage, whichever is later?	Yes	
Is the claims appeals time period defined as 12 months, or at least as long as Payer's audit time period?	Yes	
Does the contract define the proof of timely filing as a printout of the electronic claims submission screen?	Yes	
Plan agrees that it will not deny reimbursement at the acute hospital bed rate in circumstances where Plan has determined that a member can be appropriately cared for in a skilled nursing bed, but for any reason beyond Hospital's control the Plan's skilled nursing providers are unable or unwilling to accept such member, or the member is unwilling to be transferred.	Yes	
Appendix dealing with rates: It is recommended that a separate appendix be developed for each product where there are different rates involved and that these products be clearly defined. This will reduce confusion regarding payment arrangements.	Yes	
If payment rates are based on diagnosis-related group (DRG) and the contract exceeds one year in length, it should include a methodology for adjusting payment as the federal DRG grouper is changed. This will ensure that the original payment contemplated under the agreement is maintained.	Yes	

Agreement Sections (Bolded provisions are those most important.)	High Preference	HMO/ PPO
Compensation *(continued)*		
Any exclusions from the DRG or per diem rates should be clearly delineated (e.g., t-PA [revenue code 259], implants [revenue codes 275–278], trauma, Xigris [new sepsis drug]). For implants, negotiate percentage off of charges rather than cost +/−. This eliminates administrative hassles regarding invoices. Negotiate separate reimbursement for drugs costing more than $500, especially new drugs.	Yes	
Any hospital-based physician fees within the hospital rate should be clearly defined (e.g., emergency room physician's charge included in the hospital emergency room bill). General policy is NOT to include in hospital rates.	No	
Are there separate mother and baby case rates?	Yes	
Are expectant mothers on bed rest paid at the medical per diem until the mother goes into active labor, then at the obstetrics case rate?	Yes	
Is there an additional nursery per diem for multiple births?	Yes	
Are observation rates, and when they apply (e.g., automatically move to inpatient status after 23 hours and 59 minutes) defined? Clarify observation reimbursement from emergency department and outpatient surgery reimbursement. Achieve reimbursement for diagnostic tests and nonsurgical procedures performed during observation.	Yes	
Is there additional reimbursement for multiple outpatient surgeries (e.g., 100% on primary surgery, 50% on all others)?	Yes	
Is there a percentage discount on "all other inpatients and outpatients not specifically mentioned in the contract"?	Yes	
All payment terms should be clearly defined. It is suggested that revenue codes be used in the contract where appropriate to clarify what is included within what rates (e.g., surgical step-down—revenue code 206, 214).	Yes	
Is the compensation renegotiation date specified?	Yes	
Are cost of living/consumer price index adjustments in contract?	Yes	
Is there a clear definition of how coordination of benefits works? It should not apply when a government contract is primary. If an HMO is primary and a PPO/POS is secondary and Hospital is not in network for the HMO, the PPO/POS will pay the entire claim and not claim the benefit of the HMO (i.e., not to pay out-of-network claims).	Yes	
Are reimbursement rates renegotiated yearly?	Yes	
Is there a favored-nations provision in the agreement for hospital rates? Do other contracts exist with a favored-nations clause, and is this agreement consistent with those contracts? If a favored-nations provision has been agreed to, is there a clear understanding of how this provision will be applied (e.g., if rates are per diem, this contract provision only applies to other per diem arrangements; every year an independent auditor will verify Hospital is in compliance)?	No	

Agreement Sections (Bolded provisions are those most important.)	High Preference	HMO/ PPO
Compensation *(continued)*		
If sufficient evidence of coverage or referral is not presented, can Hospital hold Member financially responsible, as it is a dual responsibility of Member and Hospital?	Yes	
Is 24/7 eligibility determination available? If not, will Plan pay when reasonable efforts are made to obtain verification (e.g., use prior list of members)? Consider the following language: "Payer Organization shall provide staffing twenty-four (24) hours per day, seven (7) days per week to respond to requests for verification of Member eligibility and authorization of Covered Services. Payer Organization shall approve or deny such requests within two (2) hours, provided, however, that any decision to deny authorization due to lack of medical necessity shall be made only by a physician licensed by the State after consultation with Provider's treating physician. For approved services, Payer Organization shall also advise Provider of copayments and deductibles applicable to the Covered Services."	Yes	
Are leased networks required to price the claim within 10 calendar days?	Yes	
Are Payers required to provide notification of receipt of electronic claim to the electronic clearinghouse?	Yes	
Does Plan/Payer notify Hospital within 10 days of receipt if additional claim information is needed or absent notice the claim is deemed to be clean?	Yes	
If additional information is required, does Plan pay within ten days of receipt of this information or claim reverts to billed charges?	Yes	
Utilization Management (UM)/Quality Assurance (QA)		
Does contract provide UR/QA documentation?	Yes	
Who conducts UR?		
When will UR occur?		
What UR criteria are used?		
Is there a clause that states all communication re: UR/QA is deemed to be communication to a peer review committee and is therefore confidential under law?	Yes	
Is precertification required only by the entity to receive payment?	Yes	
Utilization review plans' essential elements: 1. All decisions to deny services shall be made by physicians. 2. Access to hospital records does not include access to UR/QA committee minutes. 3. UR program process shall be conducted in a time frame so as not to place Covered Individual in a position of not electing to receive services based on one opinion. 4. Each identification card shall clearly designate instructions and contact information pertaining to the UM agent. 5. Plan shall respond to Provider inquiries by next business day.	Yes	

Agreement Sections (Bolded provisions are those most important.)	High Preference	HMO/ PPO
Utilization Management (UM)/Quality Assurance (QA) *(continued)*		

6. Emergency admissions shall be authorized the next business day.
7. Authorization of admission is the responsibility of Provider or Covered Individual as defined by Plan.
8. Type of review, criteria set, and staffing plan shall be specified.
9. Rules required of Plan and Provider shall be stipulated.
10. Plan must abide by Facility policies governing on-site review.
11. A general outline of the following review processes shall be provided:
  • Preadmission review
  • Admission review
  • Continued stay review
  • Focused review
  • Quality assurance review
  • Discharge planning review
  • Ambulatory review
12. Direct patient access should be avoided or controlled through hospital UM departments.
13. Hospital should be able to bill patients for continued stays, with written permission of patient.
	Yes	

If a covered service is denied for no preauthorization and is later proven to be medically necessary, the claim must be reprocessed and paid at the in-network benefit level. **Recommended language**: "Facility will use best efforts to comply with Payer utilization protocols as stated in this Agreement and the Provider Manual. If Facility provides a medically necessary service to a Member and Facility fails to comply with such utilization protocols, and should Payer deny payment of a claim due to Facility's failure to comply with such utilization protocols, Facility has the right to utilize the appeals process to seek payment for the service. If (a) at the time that the service was provided it met either (i) Interqual criteria for medically necessary services or (ii) was consistent with the applicable guidelines for the appropriate professional colleges and societies or (iii) met the requirements under Medicare review policies; (b) Member was eligible on the date of service; and (c) the service was a Covered Service, Payer agrees to pay the claim according to Exhibit A of the Agreement. Thus, the appeal decision will be based solely on the criterion of medical necessity." [Note that we are disallowing any second guessing or retrospective review by the payer. If, at the time of service and with all the facts at hand at that time, the service was deemed to be medically necessary, it is considered "medically necessary." Also, we admit that the payer has the right to deny for lack of prior authorization, but upon appeal, medical necessity (defined here in relation to Interqual, professional society guidelines, and Medicare policy) becomes the only factor for consideration.]	Yes	

Agreement Sections (Bolded provisions are those most important.)	High Preference	HMO/ PPO
Term and Termination		
Is there a no-cause termination clause?	Yes	
Can Hospital terminate or not contract with selected payers?	Yes	
Are there any limitations on terminating the contract other than time?	No	
Is there an evergreen clause?	No, unless discount off of charges	
If yes, it needs to: a. define a method for renegotiating rates b. allow for renegotiation of rates during the term of the agreement. At a minimum this should occur if Plan increases the number of hospitals (or providers as defined in the agreement) in a geographic area of Hospital or Provider or if Plan carves out special services.	Yes	
Is breach-of-contract clause clearly defined (includes insolvency, late or improper payments, etc.)?	Yes	
Is there a cure period in the event of breach of contract?	Yes	
Independent Contractors		
Does the contract state that both entities are independent contractors?	Yes	
Insurance		
Does the contract state that both parties carry appropriate liability insurance?	Yes	
Medical Records		
Is access to administrative and accounting records restricted to members only?	Yes	
Access to information and records should include: a. Requirement to maintain all information regarding members and providers confidential. b. Requirement to maintain all information regarding the financial nature of the contract or business plans of either party learned as a result of the contract (e.g., at the steering committee meetings) confidential. c. Reasonable access by Plan to records necessary to monitor the performance of Provider under the contract. d. Reasonable access by government and accrediting agencies.	Yes	
Does Payer pay for all reasonable costs of Hospital or Physician complying with Payer's review of medical records?	Yes	
Confidentiality		
Is there confidential information language? Proprietary information language?	Yes	
Assignment of Agreement		
Can Payer assign agreement to another party? (90-day notice with the ability to cancel the contract. Prefer mutual consent.)	Yes	

Agreement Sections (Bolded provisions are those most important.)	High Preference	HMO/ PPO
Amendments		
Can Payer amend contract or change rates or its policies without Hospital consent (except when change is mandated by law)?	No	
If yes, can Hospital terminate contract without cause prior to the effective date of the change?	Yes	
Governing Law		
Is the contract governed by the law of the state in which the hospital is located?	Yes	
Non-Compete		
Is there non-compete language relating to offering patients other plans?	No	
Other Items		
If contracting with one of the top five or six payers, is there a steering committee from Plan and Hospital or Physician to meet at a minimum quarterly to address any operational issues or items requiring consensus? The committee should have the necessary authority to resolve these issues.	Yes	

Additional Resources

Abramowitz, K. 2004. "Consumer-Directed Health Care Won't Fly." [Online article; retrieved 1/28/05.] *Managed Care Magazine* 13 (1). http://www.managedcaremag.com/archives/0401/0401.plan2009_abramowitz.html.

Atlantic Information Services, Inc. 2004. "Six Trends in Consumer-Directed Health Plan Enrollment for 2004." [Online article; retrieved 1/28/05; member subscription only.] http://www.aishealth.com/ConsumerDirected/CDarticles/MCWTrendsCD.html.

Cross, M. 2003. "Consumer-Directed Health Care: Too Good To Be True?" [Online article; retrieved 1/28/05.] *Managed Care Magazine* 12 (9). http://www.managedcaremag.com/archives/0309/0309.cdhc_main.html.

Davis, K. 2004. "Will Consumer-Directed Health Care Improve System Performance?" [Online article; retrieved 1/28/05.] *Issue Brief (Commonwealth Fund)* (773): 1–4. http://www.cmwf.org/usr_doc/davis_cdhc-hsr_ib_773.pdf.

Diamond, F. 2001. "Defined Contribution: Why It Won't Happen Anytime Soon." [Online article; retrieved 1/28/05.] *Managed Care Magazine* 10 (2). http://www.managedcaremag.com/archives/0102/0102.defined.html.

Hibbard, J. H., J. Dubow, and E. Peters. 2003. "Decision-Making in Consumer-Directed Health Plans." [Online article; retrieved 1/28/05.] Report No. #2003-05. http://research.aarp.org/health/2003_05_cdp.pdf.

Kotin, T. 2002. "Are Consumer-Directed Health Plans Good Medicine?" [Online article; retrieved 1/28/05.] Mercer Human Resources Consulting, September 17. http://www.mercerhr.com/summary.jhtml/dynamic/idContent/1068735.

Rubenstein, S. 2004. "High-deductible Health Plans Get a Boost from Demand for HSAs." [Online article; retrieved 1/28/05; member access only.] *Wall Street Journal Online*, September 14. http://online.wsj.com/article /0,,SB109467208245312587,00.html.

U.S. Department of the Treasury. 2004. "Health Savings Accounts." [Online web page; retrieved 1/28/05.] http://www.treas.gov/offices/public-affairs/hsa/.

About the Author

Robert S. Bonney, J.D., FACHE, is currently senior vice president for business development at Saint Luke's Health System in Kansas City, Missouri. He has more than 27 years of healthcare experience, including serving simultaneously as a senior vice president of an integrated delivery system and the executive vice president and chief operating officer of the system's two largest hospitals; he served more recently as the executive director of a 170,000-member managed care company.

Mr. Bonney holds masters' degrees in both business administration and health services management from the University of Missouri–Columbia and a law degree, graduating summa cum laude, from the Detroit College of Law. He has coauthored two books, several book chapters, and numerous articles and has held faculty positions at the Harvard School of Public Health in Boston, University of Missouri–Columbia, and University of Kansas in Lawrence.

Mr. Bonney is board certified in healthcare management and a Fellow of the American College of Healthcare Executives. He has been an ACHE faculty member for 20 years and is currently teaching the ACHE course entitled, "Positioning Strategies for Health Plan Contracting: Market-Based Approaches to Buying and Selling Healthcare," which helps prepare organizations for the shift to consumer-driven healthcare.

Feel free to e-mail your comments about this book to Mr. Bonney at bob.bonney@gmail.com. It is his hope that this book provides you with one good idea as you consider the future of consumer-directed healthcare in your market.

This book is part of the Executive Essentials Book Series

Executive Essentials books provide everything you should know about a topic in a concise format. Easy to read on the run, each book features tips and tools in a straightforward layout. With Executive Essentials, you *can* fit reading into your overbooked schedule.

OTHER BOOKS IN THE EXECUTIVE ESSENTIALS SERIES

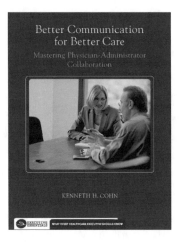

Better Communication for Better Care
Mastering Physician-Administrator Collaboration
Kenneth H. Cohn, M.D.

If you are like most healthcare professionals, you have firsthand experience of the abrasive interfaces that can occur between physicians and administrators. This book provides fresh tools and ideas for overcoming the training, outlook, and culture issues that have plagued physician-administrator relationships.

Launching a Healthcare Capital Project
John E. Kemper

You've decided to invest large amounts of time, money, and manpower in a facility expansion. Getting it done right the first time is critical, and your role is key. This book provides you with what you need to know about launching, organizing, and implementing a capital project.

For current pricing or to purchase these books online, visit
www.ache.org/hap.cfm

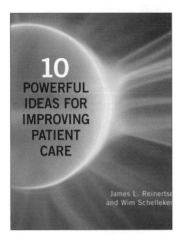

10 Powerful Ideas for Improving Patient Care
James L. Reinertsen, M.D., and Wim Schellekens, M.D.
Copublished with the Institute for Healthcare Improvement

Chosen from among hundreds of approaches, the quality improvement ideas in this book were filtered through the perspective of quality experts with clinical as well as administrative experience. Each idea is thoroughly illustrated with examples and descriptions of actual results. You will also learn what pitfalls to avoid when implementing each idea and where you can turn for more information or guidance.

Decision Making for Improved Performance
Ken E. Mack, FACHE; Mary Ann Crawford, R.N., Ph.D.; and Mary C. Reed

Slow and ineffective decision making can be costly in today's demanding healthcare environment. This hands-on, step-by-step guide will help you eliminate common mistakes in decision making. The authors have whittled the process down to seven steps, mirroring the effective decision-making approach used in clinical medicine.

Leading Others, Managing Yourself
Peter McGinn, Ph.D.

Leadership is more than having a knack for predicting trends, a head for numbers, or years of experience to draw upon; it is also about judgment, passion, and values. The best leaders know themselves, and they know the people with whom they work. This book will help you sharpen your leadership capabilities and learn how to use your insights to lead others.

For current pricing or to purchase these books online, visit
www.ache.org/hap.cfm

Leading a Patient-Safe Organization
Matthew J. Lambert III, M.D., FACHE

If you are like most executives, you delegate the details of clinical quality to the medical staff. But do you understand your critical role in developing a patient-safe organization? This book focuses on what healthcare administrators need to know about medical error and fostering a culture of safety.